W9-ARQ-549

Praise for Michael E. Gerber, Michael Steranka, and *The E-Myth Financial Advisor*

Michael Steranka has outlined how to systematize your planning practice. **This is a must-read for all advisors looking to grow their practice!**

Ed Slott, CPA, founder, IRAhelp.com

Michael Steranka has consistently demonstrated huge production levels. Mike has created a system that achieves extraordinary results. **Producers wanting to get to the next level would be well served by listening, learning, and following Mike's coaching.**

Mark Heitz, president, sales and distribution, Aviva Life and Annuity

I do not know of anyone else in the industry that has as high a level of competence in aiding clients with insurance solutions as Michael. We have had the privilege of supporting him for many years at Creative. **When Michael speaks to fellow agents, they leave with a new perspective on how to improve their practice.**

Mike Tripses, CEO, Creative Marketing

I am very proud of my brother, Mike! **I am continually impressed with his ability to explain complex financial matters in everyday terms.**

Joe Steranka, CEO, PGA of America

The E-Myth Financial Advisor provides the necessary course of action to set up a successful financial advisory firm. **I have met Mike, and he has an ability to make his ideas come to life. I strongly encourage you to read and act on his recommendations.**

Darren Root, CPA, CITP; CEO, RootWorks; co-author, *The E-Myth Accountant;* president and founder, Root & Associates

Great salesmen and great business-builders do not always come together. Mike Steranka is the exception to this rule. **Mike is not only one of the best face-to-face salesmen I have ever seen in action, but he possesses the vision to see what could be, as well as the courage to execute the plan to make dreams become reality.** Adding to his uniqueness is his ability to help others gain these valuable skills.

Douglas C. Wykoff, former CEO and marketing executive

Michael Gerber's E-Myth is one of only four books I recommend as required reading. **For those looking to start and build a business of their own, this is the man who has coached more successful entrepreneurs than the next ten gurus combined.**

Timothy Ferris, #1 New York Times best-selling author, *The 4-Hour Workweek*

Everyone needs a mentor, someone who tells it like it is, holds you accountable, and shows you your good, bad, and ugly. For millions of small business owners, Michael Gerber is that person. Let Michael be your mentor and you are in for a kick in the pants, the ride of a lifetime.

John Jantsch, author, *Duct Tape Marketing*

Michael Gerber is a master instructor and a leader's leader. As a combat F15 fighter pilot, I had to navigate complex missions with life-and-death consequences, but until I read The E-Myth and met Michael Gerber, my transition to the world of small business was a nightmare with no real flight plan. **The hands-on, practical magic of Michael's turnkey systems magnified by the raw power of his keen insight and wisdom have changed my life forever.**

Steve Olds, CEO, Stratworx.com

Michael Gerber's strategies in The E-Myth were instrumental in building my company from two employees to a global organization; I can't wait to see how applying the strategies from Awakening the Entrepreneur Within will affect its growth!

Dr. Ivan Misner, founder and chairman, BNI; author, Masters of Sales

Michael Gerber's gift to isolate the issues and present simple, direct, business-changing solutions shines bright with Awakening the Entrepreneur Within. If you're interested in developing an entrepreneurial vision and plan that inspires others to action, buy this book, read it, and apply the processes Gerber brilliantly defines.

Tim Templeton, author, The Referral of a Lifetime

Michael Gerber truly, truly understands what it takes to be a successful practicing entrepreneur and business owner. He has demonstrated to me over six years of working with him that for those who stay the course and learn much more than just "how to work on their business and not in it" then they will reap rich rewards. I finally franchised my business, and the key to unlocking this kind of potential in any business is the teachings of Michael's work.

Chris Owen, marketing director, Royal Armouries (International) PLC

My wife, Colleen, and I spent twenty-five years flying in the United States Air Force and with commercial airlines. When we changed our career focus and decided to open our own business, we read dozens of books and attended countless seminars. Nothing came close to the quality and precision of the environment that we had lived in for all those years—until we read Michael Gerber's books. His insightful writings finally gave us the flight plan that we had been missing. We carry copies of his books in our car and share them with other entrepreneurs, because we know that their lives and businesses can be changed in a profound way by the wisdom of Michael Gerber.

Bill and Colleen Hensley, founders, Hensley Properties Inc.;
authors, The Pilot-Learning Leadership

Michael's work has been an inspiration to us. His books have helped us get free from the out-of-control life that we once had. His no-nonsense approach kept us focused on our ultimate aim rather than day-to-day stresses. He has helped take our business to levels we couldn't have imagined possible. In the Dreaming Room made us totally re-evaluate how we thought about our business and our life. We have now redesigned our life so we can manifest the dreams we unearthed in Michael's Dreaming Room.

Jo and Steve Davison, founders, The Spinal Health Clinic
Chiropractic Group and www.your-dream-life.com

Rarely—maybe once in a lifetime—is there a message that transforms us, that inspires us to create the vision that describes the grandest version of ourselves, and then act upon it. Several years ago, we heard such a message, Michael Gerber's message. Since then, our journey with Michael has truly awakened the entrepreneur within us! We can't wait to take our lives and the lives of our clients to the next level through this book!

Robert and Susan Clements, principals, E-Myth Iowa

Because of Michael Gerber, I transformed my twenty-four-hour-a-day, seven-day-a-week job (also called a small business) into a multimillion turnkey business. This in turn set the foundation for my worldwide training firm. I am living my dream because of Michael Gerber.

Howard Partridge, Phenomenal Products Inc.

Michael Gerber is an outrageous revolutionary who is changing the way the world does business. He dares you to commit to your grandest dreams and then shows you how to make the impossible a reality. If you let him, this man will change your life.

Fiona Fallon, founder, Divine and The Bottom Line

Michael Gerber is a genius. Every successful business person I meet has read Michael Gerber, refers to Michael Gerber, and lives by his words. You just can't get enough of Michael Gerber. He has the innate (and rare) ability to tap into one's soul, look deeply, and tell you what you need to hear. And then, he inspires you, equips you with the tools to get it done.

Pauline O'Malley, CEO, TheRevenueBuilder

When asked "Who was the most influential person in your life?" I am one of the thousands who don't hesitate to say "Michael E. Gerber." **Michael helped transform me from someone dreaming of retirement to someone dreaming of working until age one hundred.** This awakening is the predictable outcome of anyone reading Michael's new book.

Thomas O. Bardeen

Michael Gerber is an incredible business philosopher, guru, perhaps even a seer. He has an amazing intuition, which allows him to see in an instant what everybody else is missing; he sees opportunity everywhere. **While in the Dreaming Room, Michael gave me the gift of seeing through the eyes of an awakened entrepreneur, and instantly my business changed from a regional success to serving clients on four continents.**

Keith G. Schiehl, president, Rent-a-Geek Computer Services

Michael Gerber is among the very few who truly understand entrepreneurship and small business. While others talk about these topics in the form of theories, methodologies, processes, and so on, Michael goes to the heart of the issues. **Whenever Michael writes about entrepreneurship, soak it in as it is not only good for your business, but great for your soul.** His words will help you to keep your passion and balance while sailing through the uncertain sea of entrepreneurship.

Raymond Yeh, co-author, *The Art of Business*

Michael Gerber's insight, wisdom, caring, and straightforward approach helped me reinvent myself and my business while doubling my revenues in less than one year. Crack open this book and let him do the same for you, too.

Christine Kloser, author, *The Freedom Formula and Conscious Entrepreneurs*

Michael Gerber forced me to think big, think real, and gave me the support network to make it happen. A new wave of entrepreneurs is rising, much in thanks to his amazing efforts and very practical approach to doing business.

Christian Kessner, founder, Higher Ground Retreats and Events

Michael's understanding of entrepreneurship and small business management has been a difference maker for countless businesses, including Infusion Software. **His insights into the entrepreneurial process of building a business are a must-read for every small business owner.** The vision, clarity, and leadership that came out of our Dreaming Room experience were just what our company needed to recognize our potential and motivate the whole company to achieve it.

Clate Mask, president and CEO, Infusion Software

Michael Gerber is a truly remarkable man. His steady openness of mind and ability to get to the deeper level continues to be an inspiration and encouragement to me. **He seems to always ask that one question that forces the new perspective to break open and he approaches the new coming method in a fearless way.**

Rabbi Levi Cunin, Chabad of Malibu

The Dreaming Room experience was literally life-changing for us. **Within months, we were able to start our foundation and make several television appearances owing to his teachings.** He has an incredible charisma, which is priceless, but above all Michael Gerber awakens passion from within, enabling you to take action with dramatic results . . . starting today!

Shona and Shaun Carcary, Trinity Property Investments Inc.—Home Vestors franchises

I thought E-Myth was an awkward name! What could this book do for me? **But when I finally got to reading it . . . it was what I was looking for all along.** Then, to top it off, I took a twenty-seven-hour trip to San Diego just to attend the Dreaming Room, where Michael touched my heart, my mind, and my soul.

Helmi Natto, president, Eye 2 Eye Optics, Saudi Arabia

I attended In the Dreaming Room and was challenged by Michael Gerber to "Go out and do what's impossible." So I did; **I became an author and international speaker and used Michael's principles to create a world-class company that will change and save lives all over the world.**

Dr. Don Kennedy, MBA; author, *5 AM & Already Behind*, www.bahbits.com

I went to the Dreaming Room to have Michael Gerber fix my business. He talked about Dreaming. What was this Dreaming? I was too busy working! Too busy being miserable, angry, frustrated, behind in what I was trying to accomplish. And losing everything I was working for. **Then Michael Gerber woke up the dreamer in me and remade my life and my business.**

Pat Doorn, president, Mountain View Electric Ltd.

Michael Gerber can captivate a room full of entrepreneurs and take them to a place where they can focus on the essentials that are the underpinning of every successful business. He gently leads them from where they are to where they need to be in order to change the world.

Francine Hardaway, CEO, Stealthmode Partners; founder,
the Arizona Entrepreneurship Conferences

The  Myth

Financial Advisor

Why Most Financial Advisory
Practices Don't Work
and What to Do About It

MICHAEL E. GERBER

MICHAEL STERANKA

PRODIGY
BUSINESS BOOKS

Published by
Prodigy Business Books, Inc., Carlsbad, California.

Production Team
Trish Beaulieu, book division manager, Dezign Matters Creative Group, Inc.;
Helen Chang, editor, helenchangwriter.com; Erich Broesel, cover designer,
BroselDesign, Inc.; Nancy Ratkiewich, book production, njr productions;
Jeff Kassebaum, Michael E. Gerber author photographer, Jeff Kassebaum and Co.;
Anne Gummerson, Michael Steranka co-author photographer.

For general information on other products and services, please visit the website:
www.michaelegerber.com.

ISBN: 978-0-9835001-4-8 (pbk)
ISBN: 978-0-9835001-5-5 (cloth)
ISBN: 978-0-9835542-2-6 (ebk)

Printed in the United States of America

10 9 8 7 6 5 4 3 2 1

To Luz Delia, whose heart expands mine,
whose soul inspires mine,
whose boldness reaches for the stars, thank you,
forever, for being, truly mine…

—Michael E. Gerber

CONTENTS

A Word About This Book   iii

A Note from Michael Steranka   v

Preface   ix

Acknowledgments   xiii

Introduction   xvii

Chapter 1: The Story of Steve and Peggy   1

Chapter 2: My Career . . . and Yours   9

Chapter 3: On the Subject of Money   19

Chapter 4: Money Dynamics—Seeing Is Believing   31

Chapter 5: On the Subject of Planning   41

Chapter 6: Planning Your Course   53

Chapter 7: On the Subject of Management   63

Chapter 8: Managing the Unmanageable   69

Chapter 9: On the Subject of People   73

Chapter 10: People Needing People   79

Chapter 11: On the Subject of Associates   87

Chapter 12: The Associate Financial Advisor   91

Chapter 13: On the Subject of Estimating   97

Chapter 14: Billing and Certainty   101

Chapter 15: On the Subject of Clients   107

Chapter 16: Your Clients Love You, They Love You Not   113

Chapter 17: On the Subject of Growth   119

Chapter 18: Growing Joys   123

Chapter 19: On the Subject of Change   127

Chapter 20: The Gift of Change   135

Chapter 21: On the Subject of Time   139

Chapter 22: What Time Do You Have?   145

Chapter 23: On the Subject of Work   149

Chapter 24: The Reason Behind the Work   153

Chapter 25: On the Subject of Taking Action   159

Chapter 26: Taking Action   165

Afterword   **169**
About the Authors   **171**
About the Series   **174**

A WORD ABOUT THIS BOOK

Michael E. Gerber

My first E-Myth book was published in 1985. It was called *The E-Myth: Why Most Small Businesses Don't Work and What to Do About It*. Since that book, and the company I created to provide business development services to its many readers, millions have read *The E-Myth* and the book that followed it, called *The E-Myth Revisited*, and tens of thousands have participated in our E-Myth Mastery programs.

The co-author of this book, Michael Steranka, is one of my more enthusiastic readers, and as a direct result of his enthusiasm, his financial advisory practice became one of those clients. He became, over the years, one of my friends.

This book is two things: the product of my lifelong work conceiving, developing, and growing the E-Myth way into a business model that has been applied to every imaginable kind of company in the world, as well as a product of Michael Steranka's extraordinary experience and success applying the E-Myth to development of his equally extraordinary enterprise, Retirement Planning Services, Inc.

So it was that one day, while sitting with my muse, which I think of as my inner voice, and which many who know me think of as "here he goes again!" I thought about the creation of an entire series of E-Myth Expert books. That series, including this book, would be co-authored by experts in every industry who had successfully applied my E-Myth principles to the extreme development of a practice—a very small company—with the intent of growing it nationwide, and even worldwide, which is what Michael Steranka had in mind as he began to discover the almost infinite range of opportunities provided by thinking the E-Myth way.

Upon seeing the possibilities of this new idea, I immediately invited co-authors such as Michael Steranka to join me. They said, "Let's do it!" and so we did.

Welcome to *The E-Myth Financial Advisor: Why Most Financial Advisory Practices Don't Work and What to Do About It.*

Read it, enjoy it, and let us—Michael Steranka and I—help you apply the E-Myth to the re-creation, development, and extreme growth of your financial advisory practice into an enterprise that you can be justifiably proud of.

To your life, your wisdom, and the life and success of your clients, I wish you good reading.

—Michael E. Gerber
Co-Founder/Chairman
Michael E. Gerber Companies, Inc.
Carlsbad, California
www.michaelegerber.com/co-author

A NOTE FROM MICHAEL STERANKA

In the early 1990s, I picked up a copy of an inconspicuous book entitled *The E-Myth Revisited*, by Michael E. Gerber. I would like to say I read it, implemented it, and lived happily ever after.

In fact, the book intimidated me, because although it was simple it was at the same time complex. This guy, Gerber, was talking about systematizing *everything*. Are you kidding me? Everything? This guy must be nuts or brilliant. I couldn't decide which at that point.

You see, I wasn't really ready to work *on* my business instead of *in* my business. My comprehension of just what a business is and is not was not truly clear to me. I was too busy just doing it, doing it, doing it. Sure, I set goals and yes, I achieved those goals—but was I really building a business? When you start thinking of building a business that does not involve you, then you can really think of building a business. Why? Because you are taking you out of the equation and you are forced to think about what is left. Sure, every entrepreneur has specific talents or charisma or enthusiasm. But they have much more and until they remove themselves from the equation it may be impossible for them to grasp just what separates their business from their competitors.

That is really the brilliance of the E-Myth philosophy. Removing the technician from the practice and looking at what you do outside of your narrow scope. By removing yourself you now can focus on what distinguishes your business. If it is you and only you . . . Houston, we may have a problem. What you're building should be bigger than you, bigger than any one individual. It should be system-atized so it can be duplicated and replicated.

When they say read this and reread this, it's for a purpose. The purpose is for you to force your brain to take the time to design what was divinely intended for you all along. It takes work. But the results are incredible. Michael E. Gerber has made this process even easier because he has reached out to those in their respective disci-plines who did the heavy lifting so you don't have to. Simply find the experts in your discipline who have systematized their business through E-Myth and you are light years ahead of the competition.

I remember hearing Michael speak many years ago and he said something like, what if you had to open 1,000 stores in thirty days? What would you do? How would you do it?

Do you have the systems and processes in place in order for this to happen? Would it be smooth or a nightmare? The words really resonated with me and somewhere in the back of my mind I said, "Someday I will do just what Michael said."

That someday came sooner than I thought and the opportunity was that I had just closed a huge referral source and now I had to deliver. The good news was that I had been stockpiling parts of my system over the years. Taking notes on procedures and figuring out how to systematize my practice one step at a time. So I dove into E-Myth and spent hundreds of hours documenting everything I could think about as it related to my business. The result was a system.

Since then, I have been absolutely painstaking in my approach to following the E-Myth philosophy to the letter. I have put in thou-sands of hours over the years between myself and my staff. And boy has it made my life easier. The profits have been considerably more and I am no longer perplexed. I have a system. The System, as I call it, has successfully enabled me to achieve goals that were previously unbelievable, both literally and figuratively.

So I was sitting at a restaurant in San Diego with two of the most impressive attorneys I had ever met. Robert Armstrong and Sanford Fisch, founders and owners of the American Academy of Estate Planning Attorneys, were asking about how my new systems were working so effectively. They kept on me to continue to document systems and procedures. I can't thank them enough for staying on me to do this.

In 2009, Robert and Sandy called and asked me the most amazing question. "Have you ever heard of Michael E. Gerber?" they said. Robert and Sandy went on to explain the importance of the E-Myth in their business and how instrumental it was in creating their nationally renowned American Academy of Estate Planning Attorneys. They went on to explain that they were co-authoring a book with Gerber called *The E-Myth Attorney: Why Most Legal Practices Don't Work and What to Do About It.*

Robert and Sandy went on to tell me that Gerber wanted to author *The E-Myth Financial Advisor* and they had suggested me as the financial advisor. Robert and Sandy had mentioned that they had watched my business really take off and were familiar with the systems I had implemented. I felt honored and humbled at the same time.

Michael and I spoke and met and have become good friends and he is quite remarkable.

There is no doubt in my mind that I would not have the success I have today without the E-Myth philosophy. Meeting Michael was like meeting a long-lost friend. I felt he instinctively knew me. What he knows are people and business, and more specifically, business-people. And he knows them better than any other expert I know.

I want to thank Robert and Sanford for recommending me to Michael E. Gerber and I want to thank Michael for this opportunity to share his vision through the eyes of an E-Myth financial advisor.

It cannot be emphasized enough how much heavy lifting all of the E-Myth experts have already done in their respective fields. If you are a financial advisor, this was written just for you. I know the hopes and dreams you have. I know the challenges and heartache you go through. So take a step back, keep an open mind, and read and enjoy. And then, reread.

—Michael Steranka
Founder and CEO
Retirement Planning Services, Inc.
Millersville, Maryland

PREFACE

Michael E. Gerber

I am not a financial advisor, though I have helped dozens of financial advisors reinvent their financial advisory practices over the past thirty-five years.

I like to think of myself as a thinker, maybe even a dreamer. Yes, I like to *do* things. But before I jump in and get my hands dirty, I prefer to think through what I'm going to do and figure out the best way to do it. I imagine the impossible, dream big, and then try to figure out how the impossible can become the possible. After that, it's about how to turn the possible into reality.

Over the years, I've made it my business to study how things work and how people work—specifically, how things and people work best together to produce optimum results. That means creating an organization that can do great things and achieve more than any other organization can.

This book is about how to produce the best results as a real-world financial advisor in the development, expansion, and *liberation* of your practice. In the process, you will come to understand what the practice of financial advisory services—as a *business*—is, and what it isn't. If you keep focusing on what it isn't, you're destined for failure. But if you turn your sights on what it *is*, the tide will turn.

This book, intentionally small, is about big ideas. The topics we'll be discussing in this book are the very issues that financial advisors face daily in their practice. You know what they are: money, management, clients, and many more. My aim is to help you begin the exciting process of totally transforming the way you do business. As such, I'm confident that *The E-Myth Financial Advisor* could well be the most important book on the practice of financial advisory as a business that you'll ever read.

Unlike other books on the market, my goal is not to tell you how to do the work you do. Instead, I want to share with you the E-Myth philosophy as a way to revolutionize the way you think about the work you do. I'm convinced that this new way of thinking is something financial advisors everywhere must adopt in order for their financial advisory practice to flourish during these trying times. I call it strategic thinking, as opposed to tactical thinking.

In strategic thinking, also called systems thinking, you, the financial advisor, will begin to think about your entire practice— the broad scope of it—instead of focusing on its individual parts. You will begin to see the end game (perhaps for the first time) rather than just the day-to-day routine that's consuming you—the endless, draining work I call "doing it, doing it, doing it."

Understanding strategic thinking will enable you to create a practice that becomes a successful business, with the potential to flourish as an even more successful enterprise. But in order for you to accomplish this, your practice, your business, and certainly your enterprise must work *apart* from you instead of *because* of you.

The E-Myth philosophy says that a highly successful financial advisory practice can grow into a highly successful financial advisory business, which in turn can become the foundation for an inordinately successful financial advisory enterprise that runs smoothly and efficiently *without* the financial advisor having to be in the office for ten hours a day, six days a week.

So what is "The E-Myth," exactly? The E-Myth is short for the Entrepreneurial Myth, which says that most businesses fail to fulfill their potential because most people starting their own business are not entrepreneurs at all. They're actually what I call *technicians suffering from an entrepreneurial seizure*. When technicians suffering from an entrepreneurial seizure start a financial advisory practice of their own, they almost always end up working themselves into a frenzy; their days are booked solid with appointments, one client after another. These financial advisors are burning the candle at both ends, fueled by too much coffee and too little sleep, and most of the time, they can't even stop to think.

In short, the E-Myth says that most financial advisors don't own a true business—most own a job. They're doing it, doing it, doing it, hoping like hell to get some time off, but never figuring out how to get their business to run without them. And if your business doesn't run well without you, what happens when you can't be in two places at once? Ultimately, your practice will fail.

There are a number of prestigious schools throughout the world dedicated to teaching the science of financial advisors. The problem is, they fail to teach the *business* of it. And because no one is being taught how to run a practice as a business, some financial advisors find themselves having to close their doors every year. You could be a world-class expert in money management or timing the market or guessing right on the price of crude, but when it comes to building a successful business, all that specified knowledge matters exactly zilch.

The good news is that you don't have to be among the statistics of failure in the financial advisory profession. The E-Myth philosophy I am about to share with you in this book has been successfully applied to many financial advisory practices just like yours with extraordinary results.

The key to transforming your practice—and your life—is to grasp the profound difference between going to work *on* your practice (systems thinker) and going to work *in* your practice (tactical thinker). In other words, it's the difference between going to work on your practice as an entrepreneur and going to work in your practice as a financial advisor.

The two are not mutually exclusive. In fact, they are essential to each other. The problem with most financial advisory practices is that the systems thinker—the entrepreneur—is completely absent. And so is the vision.

The E-Myth philosophy says that the key to transforming your practice into a successful enterprise is knowing how to transform yourself from successful financial advisory technician into successful technician-manager-entrepreneur. In the process, everything you do in your financial advisory practice will be transformed. The door is then open to turning it into the kind of practice it should be—a practice, a business, an enterprise of pure joy.

The E-Myth not only *can* work for you, it *will* work for you. In the process, it will give you an entirely new experience of your business and beyond.

To your future and your life. Good reading.

—Michael E. Gerber
Co-Founder/Chairman
Michael E. Gerber Companies, Inc.
Carlsbad, California
www.michaelegerber.com/co-author

ACKNOWLEDGMENTS

Michael E. Gerber

As always, and never to be forgotten, there are those who give of themselves to make my work possible.

To my dearest and most forgiving partner, wife, friend, and co-founder, Luz Delia Gerber, whose love and commitment takes me to places I would often not go unaccompanied.

To Jim Taylor, whose persistency and at times demonic, steady state of heart, made the impossible less improbable, and the possible, if not easy, more predictable than we hoped.

To Helen Chang, noble warrior, editor, brave soul, and sojourner, who covers all the bases we would have missed had she not been there. To Erich Broesel, our stand-alone graphic designer and otherwise visual genius who supported the creation of all things visual that will forever be all things Gerber, we thank you, deeply, for your continuous contribution of things both temporal and eternal. To Trish Beaulieu, wow, you are splendid. And to Nancy Ratkiewich, whose work has been essential for you who are reading this.

To Johanna Nilsson, who told us that social media was much, much more than just social, and then, with the grace G-d gave her, proved it every step of the way.

To those many, many dreamers, thinkers, storytellers, and leaders, whose travels with me in The Dreaming Room have given me life, breath, and pleasure unanticipated before we met. To those many participants in my life (you know who you are), thank you for taking me seriously, and joining me in this exhilarating quest.

And, of course, to my co-authors, all of you, your genius, wisdom, intelligence, and wit have supplied me with a grand view of the world, which would never have been the same without you.

Love to all.

ACKNOWLEDGMENTS

Michael Steranka

I would like to thank my family members, all of whom have contributed to this book by forming the individual I am today. My father, Joe Steranka, who instilled a work ethic in me that knows no bounds and my mother, Dorthy Steranka, who always believed in me. My brothers, Joe, John, and Pat, for paving the way for me in the world and continually giving me real-life examples to live up to and my sister, Stephanie, for her unconditional love throughout my life.

Professionally, the three people I wish to thank are Jim Adkins, Ron Rothgeb, and R. Ronald Sinclair. Although they started as professional associates, they developed into my most personal relationships. Jim Adkins was my general manager at the New York Life office in Chevy Chase, Maryland, and was the first person to tell me I was going to be a big producer. Ronny Rothgeb brought me in to the business and was one of my closest friends until his passing. Ronny was an excellent individual and I always wanted to be like Ron. My third friend, Ron Sinclair, was an attorney, a friend, and the ultimate confidante and we enjoyed many fine times together. Ron Sinclair has passed, but his memory lives on in his many fine accomplishments and huge family.

A special note to Jane Sinclair, Ron's daughter and president of Retirement Planning Services, Inc. Jane's vision was instrumental in the systems we have successfully implemented in our practice. My accomplishments would not have been possible without the support and encouragement of Ms. Sinclair. Love you, Jane.

INTRODUCTION

Michael E. Gerber

A s I write this book, the recession continues to take its toll on American businesses. Like any other industry, financial advisory services are not immune. Financial advisors all over the country are watching as clients defer visits for investment advice and retirement planning. At a time when per capita disposable income is at an all-time low, many people are choosing not to spend their hard-earned money on financial advisory services for themselves and even for their children. As a result, financial advisory service moves from the realm of necessity to luxury, and regrettably, financial planning becomes expendable.

Faced with a struggling economy and fewer and fewer clients, many financial advisors I've met are asking themselves, "Why did I ever become a financial advisor in the first place?"

And it isn't just a money problem. After thirty-five years of working with small businesses, many of them financial advisory practices, I'm convinced that the dissatisfaction experienced by countless financial advisors is not just about money. To be frank, the recession doesn't deserve all the blame, either. While the financial crisis our country is facing certainly hasn't made things any better, the problem started long before the economy tanked. Let's dig a little deeper. Let's go back to school.

Can you remember that far back? Whichever university or college of financial advisory you attended, you probably had some great teachers who helped you become the fine financial advisor you are. These schools

xviii   *The E-Myth Financial Advisor*

excel at teaching the science of financial advisory services; they'll teach you everything you need to know about modern portfolio theory, asset allocation, rebalancing your portfolio, and surviving down markets. But what they *don't* teach is the consummate skill set needed to be a successful financial advisor, and they certainly don't teach what it takes to build a successful financial advisory enterprise.

Obviously, something is seriously wrong. The education that financial advisory professionals receive in school doesn't go far enough, deep enough, broad enough. Colleges of financial advisory services don't teach you how to relate to the *enterprise* of financial advisory or to the *business* of financial advisory services; they only teach you how to relate to the *practice* of financial advisory services. In other words, they merely teach you how to be an *effective* rather than a *successful* financial advisor. Last time I checked, they weren't offering degrees in success.

That's why most financial advisors are effective, but few are successful. Although a successful financial advisor must be effective, an effective financial advisor does not have to be—and in most cases isn't—successful.

An effective financial advisor is capable of executing his or her duties with as much certainty and professionalism as possible.

A successful financial advisor, on the other hand, works balanced hours, has little stress, leads rich and rewarding relationships with friends and family, and has an economic life that is diverse, fulfilling, and shows a continuous return on investment.

A successful financial advisor finds time and ways to give back to the community but at little cost to his or her sense of ease.

A successful financial advisor is a leader, not simply someone who teaches clients how to care for themselves and protect their health, but a sage; a rich person (in the broadest sense of the word); a strong father, mother, wife, or husband; a friend, teacher, mentor, and spiritually grounded human being; and a person who can see clearly into all aspects of what it means to lead a fulfilling life.

So let's go back to the original question. Why did you become a financial advisor? Were you striving to just be an effective one, or did you dream about real and resounding success?

I don't know how you've answered that question in the past, but I am confident that once you understand the strategic thinking laid out in this book, you will answer it differently in the future.

If the ideas here are going to be of value to you, it's critical that you begin to look at yourself in a different, more productive way. I am suggesting that you go beyond the mere technical aspects of your daily job as a financial advisor and begin instead to think strategically about your financial advisory service as both a business and an enterprise.

I often say that most *practices* don't work—the people who own them do. In other words, most financial advisory practices are jobs for the financial advisors who own them. Does this sound familiar? The financial advisor, overcome by an entrepreneurial seizure, has started his or her own practice, become his or her own boss, and now works for a lunatic!

The result: The financial advisor is running out of time, patience, and ultimately money. Not to mention paying the worst price anyone can pay for the inability to understand what a true practice is, what a true business is, and what a true enterprise is—the price of his or her life.

In this book I'm going to make the case for why you should think differently about what you do and why you do it. It isn't just the future of your financial advisory practice that hangs in the balance. It's the future of your life.

The E-Myth Financial Advisor is an exciting departure from my other sole-authored books. In this book, Michael Steranka, an E-Myth expert—a licensed financial advisor who has successfully applied the E-Myth to the development of his financial advisory practice—is sharing his secrets about how he achieved extraordinary results using the E-Myth paradigm. In addition to the time-tested E-Myth strategies and systems I'll be sharing with you, you'll benefit from the wisdom, guidance, and practical tips provided by Michael, who has been in your shoes.

The problems that afflict financial advisory practices today don't only exist in the field of finance; the same problems are confronting every organization of every size, in every industry in every country in the world. *The E-Myth Financial Advisor* is next in a series of E-Myth Expert books that serves as a launching pad for Michael E. Gerber Partners™ to bring a legacy of expertise to small, struggling businesses in *all* industries. This series offers an exciting opportunity to understand and apply the significance of E-Myth methodology in both theory and practice to businesses in need of development and growth.

The E-Myth says that only by conducting your business in a truly innovative and independent way will you ever realize the unmatched joy that comes from creating a truly independent business, a business that works *without* you rather than *because* of you.

The E-Myth says that it is only by learning the difference between the work of a *business* and the business of *work* that financial advisors will be freed from the predictable and often overwhelming tyranny of the unprofitable, unproductive routine that consumes them on a daily basis.

The E-Myth says that what will make the ultimate difference between the success or failure of your financial advisory practice is first and foremost how you *think* about your business, as opposed to how hard you work in it.

So, let's think it through together. Let's think about those things—work, clients, money, time—that dominate the world of financial advisors everywhere.

Let's talk about planning. About growth. About management. About getting a life!

Let's think about improving you and your family's life through the development of an extraordinary practice. About getting the life you've always dreamed of but never thought you could actually have.

Envision the future you want, and the future is yours.

CHAPTER

1

The Story of Steve and Peggy

Michael E. Gerber

*You leave home to seek your fortune and, when you get it, you go home
and share it with your family.*

—Anita Baker

Every business is a family business. To ignore this truth is to
court disaster.

This is true whether or not family members actually work
in the business. Whatever their relationship with the business, every
member of a financial advisor's family will be greatly affected by the
decisions a financial advisor makes about the business. There's just
no way around it.

Unfortunately, like most businessmen, financial advisors tend to
compartmentalize their lives. They view their practice as a profession—
what they do—and therefore it's none of their family's business.

"This has nothing to do with you," says the financial advisor to
his wife, with blind conviction. "I leave work at the office and family
at home."

And with equal conviction, I say, "Not true!"

In actuality, your family and financial advisory practice are inextricably linked to one another. What's happening in your practice is also happening at home. Consider the following and ask yourself if each is true:

- If you're angry at work, you're also angry at home.
- If you're out of control in your financial advisory practice, you're equally out of control at home.
- If you're having trouble with money in your practice, you're also having trouble with money at home.
- If you have communication problems in your practice, you're also having communication problems at home.
- If you don't trust in your practice, you don't trust at home.
- If you're secretive in your practice, you're equally secretive at home.

And you're paying a huge price for it!

The truth is that your practice and your family are one—and you're the link. Or you should be. Because if you try to keep your practice and your family apart, if your practice and your family are strangers, you will effectively create two separate worlds that can never wholeheartedly serve each other. Two worlds that split each other apart.

Let me tell you the story of Steve and Peggy Walsh.

The Walshes met in college. They were in the same economics class, Steve a finance major and Peggy pre-med. When their discussions started to wander beyond Keynesian theory or multinational corporations and into their personal lives, they discovered they had a lot in common. By the end of the course, they weren't just talking in class; they were talking on the phone every night . . . and *not* about economics.

Steve thought Peggy was absolutely brilliant, and Peggy considered Steve the most passionate man she knew. It wasn't long before they were engaged and planning their future together. A month after graduation, they were married in a lovely garden ceremony in Peggy's childhood home.

While Steve studied at a prestigious college of financial advisory services, Peggy attended a prestigious medical school nearby. Over the next few years, the couple worked hard to keep their finances afloat. They worked long hours and studied constantly; they were often exhausted and struggled to make ends meet. But through it all, they were committed to what they were doing and to each other.

After passing his securities, life/health, and registered investment advisor exams, Steve became a financial planner in a busy practice while Peggy completed her residency. Soon afterward, the couple had their first son, and Peggy decided to take some time off to be with him. Those were good years. Steve and Peggy loved each other very much, were active members in their church, participated in community organizations, and spent quality time together. The Walshes considered themselves one of the most fortunate families they knew.

But work became troublesome. Steve grew increasingly frustrated with the way the practice was run. "I want to go into business for myself," he announced one night at the dinner table. "I want to start my own practice."

Steve and Peggy spent many nights talking about the move. Was it something they could afford? Did Steve really have the skills necessary to make a financial advisory practice a success? Were there enough clients to go around? What impact would such a move have on Peggy's career at the local hospital, their lifestyle, their son, their relationship? They asked all the questions they thought they needed to answer before Steve went into business for himself . . . but they never really drew up a concrete plan.

Finally, tired of talking and confident that he could handle whatever he might face, Steve committed to starting his own financial advisory practice. Because she loved and supported him, Peggy agreed, offering her own commitment to help in any way she could. So Steve quit his job, took out a second mortgage on their home, and leased a small office nearby.

In the beginning, things went well. A building boom had hit the town, and new families were pouring into the area. Steve had no trouble getting new clients. His practice expanded, quickly outgrowing his office.

Within a year, Steve had employed an office manager, Clarissa, to run the front desk and handle the administrative side of the business. He also hired a bookkeeper, Tim, to handle the finances. Steve was ecstatic with the progress his young practice had made. He celebrated by taking his wife and son on vacation to Italy.

Of course, managing a business was more complicated and time-consuming than working for someone else. Steve not only supervised all the jobs Clarissa and Tim did, but also was continually looking for work to keep everyone busy. When he wasn't scanning financial advisory journals to stay abreast of what was going on in the field or fulfilling continuing-education requirements to stay current on the standards of financial services, he was going to the bank, wading through client paperwork, or speaking with insurance companies (which usually degenerated into *arguing* with insurance companies). He also found himself spending more and more time on the telephone dealing with client concerns and nurturing relationships.

As the months went by and more and more clients came through the door, Steve had to spend even more time just trying to keep his head above water.

By the end of its second year, the practice, now employing two full-time and two part-time people, had moved to a larger office downtown. The demands on Steve's time had grown with the practice.

He began leaving home earlier in the morning and returning later at night. He drank more. He rarely saw his son anymore. For the most part, Steve was resigned to the problem. He saw the hard work as essential to building the "sweat equity" he had long heard about.

Money was also becoming a problem for Steve. Although the practice was growing like crazy, money always seemed scarce when it was really needed. He had discovered that he did not understand the complexity of getting paid from different vendors. Sure, he got paid quickly for securities –commissions would hit his ledger daily – but some insurance carriers only released commissions after the client had signed the policy delivery receipt. In some cases he didn't get paid for well over a month.

When Steve had worked for somebody else, he had been paid twice a month. In his own practice, he often had to wait—sometimes for months. He was still owed money on billings he had completed more than ninety days before.

When he complained to the insurance companies, it fell on deaf ears. They would shrug, smile, and say that had always been the way they did it. Of course, no matter how slowly Steve got paid, he still had to pay *his* people. This became a relentless problem. Steve often felt like a juggler dancing on a tightrope. A fire burned in his stomach day and night.

To make matters worse, Steve began to feel that Peggy was insensitive to his troubles. Not that he often talked to his wife about the practice. "Business is business" was Steve's mantra. "It's my responsibility to handle things at the office and Peggy's responsibility to take care of her own job and the family."

Peggy was working late hours at the hospital, and they'd brought in a nanny to help with their son. Steve couldn't help but notice that his wife seemed resentful, and her apparent lack of understanding baffled him. Didn't she see that he had a practice to take care of? That he was doing it all for his family? Apparently not.

As time went on, Steve became even more consumed and frustrated by his practice. When he went off on his own, he remembered saying, "I don't like people telling me what to do." But people were still telling him what to do. On one particularly frustrating morning, his office had to change an annuity contract that was issued incorrectly. The company had misspelled the client's name even though Steve had spelled it correctly on the application. He apprehensively remembered that when he had obtained this client, she had said her previous advisor's inability to change her address on an old account was one of the reasons she changed advisors. After keeping Steve on hold for twenty-five minutes on a long-distance call, the company said it had to reissue the contract, which would take three to five business days. Steve was furious.

Not surprisingly, Peggy grew more frustrated by her husband's lack of communication. She cut back on her own hours at the hospital to focus on their family, but her husband still never seemed to be around. Their relationship grew tense and strained. The rare moments they *were* together were more often than not peppered by long silences—a far cry from the heartfelt conversations that had characterized their relationship's early days, when they'd talk into the wee hours of the morning.

Meanwhile, Tim, the bookkeeper, was also becoming a problem for Steve. Tim never seemed to have the financial information Steve needed to make decisions about payroll, client billing, and general operating expenses, let alone how much money was available for Steve and Peggy's living expenses.

When questioned, Tim would shift his gaze to his feet and say, "Listen, Steve, I've got a lot more to do around here than you can imagine. It'll take a little more time. Just don't press me, okay?"

Overwhelmed by his own work, Steve usually backed off. The last thing Steve wanted was to upset Tim and have to do the books himself. He could also empathize with what Tim was going through, given the practice's growth over the past year.

Late at night in his office, Steve would sometimes recall his first years out of school. He missed the simple life he and his family had shared. Then, as quickly as the thoughts came, they would vanish. He had work to do and no time for daydreaming. "Having my own practice is a great thing," he would remind himself. "I simply have to apply myself, as I did in school, and get on with the job. I have to work as hard as I always have when something needed to get done."

Steve began to live most of his life inside his head. He began to distrust his people. They never seemed to work hard enough or to care about his practice as much as he did. If he wanted to go get something done, he usually had to do it himself.

Then one day, the office manager, Clarissa, quit in a huff, frustrated by the amount of work that her boss was demanding of her. Steve was left with a desk full of papers and a telephone that wouldn't stop ringing.

Clueless about the work Clarissa had done, Steve was over-whelmed by having to pick up the pieces of a job he didn't understand. His world turned upside down. He felt like a stranger in his own practice.

Why had he been such a fool? Why hadn't he taken the time to learn what Clarissa did in the office? Why had he waited until now?

Ever the trouper, Steve plowed into Clarissa's job with every-thing he could muster. What he found shocked him. Clarissa's work space was a disaster area! Her desk drawers were a jumble of papers, coins, pens, pencils, rubber bands, envelopes, business cards, fee slips, eye drops, and candy.

"What was she thinking?" Steve raged.

When he got home that night, even later than usual, he got into a shouting match with Peggy. He settled it by storming out of the house to get a drink. Didn't anybody understand him? Didn't anybody care what he was going through?

He returned home only when he was sure Peggy was asleep. He slept on the couch and left early in the morning, before anyone was awake. He was in no mood for questions or arguments.

When Steve got to his office the next morning, he immediately headed for the makeshift kitchen, nervously looking for some Tylenol to get rid of his throbbing headache.

What lessons can we draw from Steve and Peggy's story? I've said it once and I'll say it again: Every business is a family business. Your business profoundly touches all members of your family, even if they never set foot inside your office. Every business either gives to the family or takes from the family, just as individual family members do.

If the business takes more than it gives, the family is always the first to pay the price.

In order for Steve to free himself from the prison he created, he would first have to admit his vulnerability. He would have to confess to himself and his family that he really didn't know enough about his own practice and how to grow it.

Steve tried to do it all himself. Had he succeeded, had the practice supported his family in the style he imagined, he would have burst with pride. Instead, Steve unwittingly isolated himself, thereby achieving the exact opposite of what he sought.

He destroyed his life—and his family's life along with it.

Repeat after me: *Every business is a family business.*

Are you like Steve? I believe that all financial advisors share a common soul with him. You must learn that a business is only a business. It is not your life. But it is also true that your business can have a profoundly negative impact on your life unless you learn how to do it differently than most financial advisors do it—and definitely differently than Steve did it.

Steve's financial advisory practice could have served his and his family's life. But for that to happen, he would have had to learn how to master his practice in a way that was completely foreign to him.

Instead, Steve's practice consumed him. Because he lacked a true understanding of the essential strategic thinking that would have allowed him to create something unique, Steve and his family were doomed from day one.

This book contains the secrets that Steve should have known. If you follow in Steve's footsteps, prepare to have your life and business fall apart. But if you apply the principles we'll discuss here, you can avoid a similar fate.

Let's start with the subject of *money*. But, before we do, let's listen to the financial advisor's view about the story I just told you. Let's talk about Michael Steranka's career . . . and yours. ✤

My Career...
and Yours

Michael Steranka

So you think that money is the root of all evil. Have you ever asked what is the root of all money?

—Ayn Rand

Here's how my career in financial services nearly ended before it began.

My boss at New York Life Insurance Co. called me in to say, "You're not working out very well here."

I told him I was trying, and he said, "Well, you need to try harder."

"I don't know that I can try any harder," I said.

"Then maybe you're not cut out for this," he said. "Maybe you should go back to doing whatever you were doing before you got here."

Before I was at New York Life, I was in retail management. And I wasn't cut out for that. I knew I absolutely did not want to go back.

So I made up my mind to devour the next thirty days of work. I told myself that if my quota was to make ten appointments a week, then I would aim to make twenty. I would do this for one month, and if I failed, then I would get out because maybe my boss was correct. Maybe I wasn't cut out for this line of work.

During that month, I ended up with about sixteen appointments each week, which is a ton. I had sixty-four new appointments!

Then one night, I went out and asked all eight people there to buy the product I was selling. Everybody bought. I was eight for eight, and I made $5,000 in four hours.

At that moment, I thought, *Holy smokes, it's not that hard*. And I never looked back.

But what's frightening is this: I was inches away from giving up.

Natural Talent versus Learned Ability

So what happened? Was I born good? Did I suddenly acquire years of knowledge in just those thirty days? Or did lightning strike to give me eight for eight, and all of a sudden, success exploded out of pure luck?

If you're anything like me, then you picked up this book because you hope, as I had hoped, that you have what it takes.

The difference between myself then and myself now is that now I know that I do have what it takes. In fact, I know that everybody already has the necessary tools. You have those tools just as I have them. The question is, what will you choose to do with them?

Your most important tool is your self-confidence. Your attitude. All you have to do is provide the service your clients are paying for. When you provide the service, the money will come. It's not money that brings the success. It's the successful completion of your responsibilities, and when that happens, and then and only then, the money shows up. This idea is strange and counterintuitive, but what I mean is that first, you have to act the part.

A salesperson already knows that he has the ability to sell. Otherwise, his company never would have hired him. But if you're a salesperson, you have to position your product—or in your case, your services—in such a manner that people will acknowledge that what you're offering is pretty good. You lead them into a place in which they can say, "You're right."

When you have self-confidence, you take that affirmation of your position and make the sale. You don't say, "Well, let me tell you more" or accidentally talk yourself out of the sale.

But once you taste success, what will you do with it? Some people receive a measure of success and then they rest on their laurels and say, "I can get a big ticket any time I want." These people stop prospecting, stop marketing, and stop learning.

Never stop growing. I often read five or ten books a month. I may not finish most of them, but when I pick up something, I absorb it. Then, when I see somebody, I say, with much excitement, "I was just reading this book last night! And it's fantastic!"

Why do I do that? People are attracted to energy. If you have energy, people will gravitate to you and to the concepts that you say are fantastic. No matter what you're promoting, it's important to remember that you're not selling the product. You're selling the idea.

If I asked you to buy a product, you'd say, "What do I want from that?" But if I planted in you an idea of how that product can work in your life, you'd tell me, "Hey! That's what I want!"

In addition to confidence, the key to success is to know what to say and what not to say. Every product and every service promoted by Company A is very similar to every product and service of Company B. The main difference is the delivery, or how you pitch yourself.

When you graduated from college and researched career paths, you initially may not have considered a sales profession in the financial services industry. Maybe you imagined your parents would scoff at the idea and say, "Sales? Why did you spend money on higher education if you were just going to sell something?"

But those of us in the business understand that a profession in the financial services is a much nobler one than the stereotypical "sales" profession.

Picture the first time you opened your box of business cards. You looked at your name, you saw with whom you were affiliated, and you believed you had arrived. Who cares that you didn't know the first thing about formulating a business plan? You'd pick up what you needed to know as you went along. Or the company you work for would reveal everything you'd need to know about starting a business. Right?

Not exactly.

When someone is new to our industry, whoever recruited that individual sits down with him or her and talks about all the wonderful possibilities in the financial services. Chances are, that recruiter is someone in a managerial-type position and has no clue how to make those possibilities a reality.

Then when business is fruitless and the producer hasn't met his expectations, he approaches his manager and asks, "How do I increase my sales? How do I attract better clients?" And the manager, half the time, has no idea whatsoever.

So now, our sales guy is extremely frustrated. He looks at how hard he labors in relation to what little success he sees, and wonders, "What did I get myself into?"

And on top of that, the manager is probably saying, "You better figure it out if you want to stay here."

Sound familiar?

When I began working as an agent at a career agency shop in New York Life, I increased my sales dramatically through the actions I personally took to invest more in myself and in my business.

Then my sales manager had the nerve to tell me, "Next year, I want you to increase these sales by 30 percent." This happened when I was increasing the sales myself without any support from him!

In any company in the financial services sector—whether you're recruited by Ameriprise or New York Life or Merrill Lynch—you most often get a phonebook and two words: "Start calling." You're even asked to write a list of one hundred of your relatives and friends to start prospecting them.

Approximately 95 percent of new recruits in the financial services are washed out during the first three years.

We've got a system in which we gather the best and the brightest of college graduates or business school graduates and pair them with the best and the brightest of the financial institutions, and yet the success rate is dismal.

This failure rate occurs when these newbies are forced to transition to a 100 percent commission and fees-generated career. At that point, only the strong survive, plus the others who are spoon-fed accounts or take over accounts because they know somebody. But most people don't know somebody. So all of a sudden, they can eat only what they kill. Since they can't kill enough to eat, they leave the business. Meanwhile, most of these companies are not inclined to do enough effective marketing on behalf of their field force, so they can't help bring in the number of accounts needed to put something on everybody's plate.

It will only become harder for anyone to enter our profession because that person not only needs to be intelligent and highly educated; he or she also will need money.

The truth of the matter is that we still have to pay our bills. We have to invest in our business through marketing, staffing, technology, and management. It's enough to make your head spin.

You and I spent a lot of time in college studying for all those exams to get us to where we wanted to be. We scored high marks. We were obviously destined for success. But running a business was the furthest thing from our minds. We became financial advisors with our hearts set on helping the world become a better place. With our education and training in tow, we marched forward with high ideals and an even higher ambition to make our mark in the marketplace.

In some ways, that was naive. It's naive to believe that we're not subject to the daily grind of business management. But we were trained technicians. How could we be expected to know about running a business? And who could help us?

A technically trained financial advisor may be able to guide you through life's financial mine fields, but will be ill-equipped to help you understand the business aspect of the marketplace. Some financial advisors aspire to management for this very reason. They think that once the heat is off from having to produce new clients, they can kick back and get a regular paycheck simply by telling other advisors what they are doing wrong. Or they think that now that they're in management, they can finally focus on the business side. God forbid they should ever have to produce and be a manager at the same time!

Every businessperson experiences the challenges of finding new clients and delivering a great product or service while managing people and maintaining a home life. You and I aren't exempt from these struggles.

The 95 percent washout rate for new financial advisors suggests that it is even more difficult for us to tackle these challenges. Brokers, registered representatives, and insurance agents sometimes trade affiliations like baseball cards. How can this be good for the companies they represent? In short, it can't be.

Companies often approach their top producers and ask, "What are you doing that's working?"

What am I doing? I'm spending money. My own money. Some strategies I've tried work. Some don't. But I constantly spend money to try new things. To make it in this industry, we have to be people who constantly grow professionally with regard to the services we offer and also market ourselves effectively and continually. We have to push ourselves to do what works for us personally.

When I started out at New York Life, I had to make cold calls to make the required ten appointments each week. I dreaded our Monday night "phone clinics," when many of these cold calls would take place. I would even stutter on the phone because I was that nervous. Those sessions were pure torture for me. I'm not a tele-marketer and I'm not good on the phone. Some people prefer the phone, but I prefer to meet people in person.

Eventually, I asked one of the guys running the phone clinic what I needed to do in order to avoid the sessions altogether. He told me that if I came into the office with ten appointments, I wouldn't be forced to attend any more clinics.

Done!

I drafted a solicitation letter, made copies, and vowed to walk into every business in Maryland, northern Virginia, and

Washington, D.C., to hand out that letter and ask to speak to the business owner.

I made it a point to try to hand out fifty to a hundred letters a day. Some days, this was effective, but on other days, I didn't pass out as many letters as I would have hoped. But the results were excellent.

On average, I picked up two direct-mail responses and two call-ins, and made two face-to-face appointments each day. So I ended up with about six leads a day, which was thirty leads over the course of the week, which then translated to more appointments than I needed. I said good-bye to phone clinics for good.

Because this method worked for me, I kept at it and even had other people hand out letters on my behalf. Then I would meet with a business owner—let's call him Joe—and say, "I made an appointment with Bob, your neighbor. I'm coming to see him next Tuesday at nine. Can I see you at eight forty-five or nine-fifteen? I just need ten to fifteen minutes of your time." Then Joe would suggest 8:45.

Then I'd go to Bob. And I'd say, "Bob, I just made an appointment with your neighbor, Joe, for eight forty-five on Tuesday. Could I come see you at nine or eight thirty?"

Set up choices and make them choose. Set appointments. I knew those appointments were what I needed because I knew that I could dress up well and present myself in front of people in ways I couldn't over the phone.

When I wasn't able to set appointments, I got by with the attitude that it was still nice to meet other businesspeople in the community. In 1991, through this routine of selling group health insurance and Key Person life insurance, I was able to establish 125 business accounts in a little over a year, which increased my residuals to about $12,000 a month.

The question you're asking by now is, "Can I do this, too? Can I transform what looks like the road to failure into an onramp for success? Or is that life reserved for the Mark McGwires of the world—those who've got bigger wrists than the next guy?"

If you're not as successful as you want to be, you belong to one of two camps. The people in the first camp recognize that they're in pain and they know they need to do something about it. Those in the other camp are either in denial or they just don't get it.

The fact that you picked up this book signals to me that you recognize that you're in pain. You've scouted other successful people and you can't seem to put your finger on how that other guy gets it done. Or you are doing well but want to increase your production. You want to know what secret he has that you don't have.

First, you have to understand that some people who have gone before you have actually taken the time to map out this process. Your next step is to decide whether you want to spend the time, energy, and resources to map out that road yourself or you want to go to somebody who's already done it.

You're reading this now because you know I've done it. I've been there. And I get it. I understand that you're inundated with service calls. You're not returning calls promptly and you feel guilty. You're anxious because you don't know whether the economy is going up or down or sideways. You can't predict what will happen with the stock market or even the bond market. And you're frustrated.

Maybe at the broker-dealer level, you feel handcuffed by compliance departments. Too many people are telling you that you can't say this and that, so you wonder how you'll ever market again. You've become disillusioned about seminars, and maybe you don't think you have what it takes to market through seminars and use them as launching pads with your existing clientele or new prospects.

We are financial advisors who try our best to morph our expertise into thriving businesses. But it's not easy.

We make a few dollars and then need to spend a few more dollars. We work long hours and into our nights and weekends just to get the job done. We carry our concerns home and our spouses ask, "What gives?"

I know. You'd give anything for a thirty-hour day.

And yet, for what? The harder we work, the less money we seem to make. Our dream job looks like a horror movie and we dread the office. Nobody appreciates or is aware of the sacrifices we make. The market rallies, then tanks. Rinse, repeat.

And we question why the retention rate is only 5 percent.

The sad fact is that most financial advisors I've encountered over the years have turned their passion into a "job." And a low-paying one at that. As Michael E. Gerber likes to say, "If you're self-employed, you're working for a lunatic."

When we first started out in the business, we wore a thousand hats. We did everything to make a small profit. And if we were smart, we reinvested a substantial amount of that profit back into the business. We hired staff. Acquired more office space. Acquired better technology. Added management. Set up a payroll. So on and so forth.

But if you're doing the same work now that you did fifteen years ago, then something is wrong. You're wearing all those hats, but some hats aren't meant to be worn by you for your whole life. And if you're like I was, you're wondering how you got to this place. You're distraught because you just spent the afternoon fiddling with the broken copy machine—something you have no business doing.

How in the world did you wind up there? And how do you get out? Why are you struggling over a ten-dollar-an-hour job instead of doing the two-*hundred*-dollar-an-hour or the two-*thousand*-dollar-an-hour job you're meant to do?

I have good news for you. It's possible to spend time with your family on vacation and effectively grow your firm.

After twenty years in the financial services industry, I can tell you that there's a way to manage and take control of all that time being stolen from you. I understand what you've been through, and I also understand how you have to adapt, change, grow, and learn in order to thrive.

So how do you do it? How do you evolve from a crazy madman to a true business professional? The E-Myth way is your golden ticket. This is a perfect time to hear what Michael E. Gerber has to teach us about money. ❖

CHAPTER

3

On the Subject of Money

Michael E. Gerber

There are three faithful friends: an old wife, an old dog, and ready money.

—Benjamin Franklin

Had Steve and Peggy first considered the subject of *money* as we will here, their lives could have been radically different.

Money is on the tip of every financial advisor's tongue, on the edge (or at the very center) of every financial advisor's thoughts, intruding on every part of a financial advisor's life.

With money consuming so much energy, why do so few financial advisors handle it well? Why was Steve, like so many financial advisors, willing to entrust his financial affairs to a relative stranger? Why is money scarce for most financial advisors? Why is there less money than expected? And yet the demand for money is *always* greater than anticipated.

What is it about money that is so elusive, so complicated, so difficult to control? Why is it that every financial advisor I've ever met

19

hates to deal with the subject of money? Why are they almost always too late in facing money problems? And why are they constantly obsessed with the desire for more of it?

Money—you can't live with it and you can't live without it. But you better understand it and get your people to understand it. Because until you do, money problems will eat your practice for lunch.

You don't need an accountant or financial planner to do this. You simply need to prod your people to relate to money very personally. From the receptionist to the planner conducting service calls, they all should understand the financial impact of what they do every day in relationship to the profit and loss of the practice.

And so you must teach your people to think like owners, not like technicians or office managers or receptionists. You must teach them to operate like personal profit centers, with a sense of how their work fits in with the practice as a whole.

You must involve everyone in the practice with the topic of money—how it works, where it goes, how much is left, and how much everybody gets at the end of the day. You also must teach them about the four kinds of money created by the practice.

The Four Kinds of Money

In the context of owning, operating, developing, and exiting from a financial advisory practice, money can be split into four distinct but highly integrated categories:

- Income
- Profit
- Flow
- Equity

Failure to distinguish how the four kinds of money play out in your practice is a surefire recipe for disaster.

Important Note: Do not talk to your accountants or book-keepers about what follows; it will only confuse them and you. The information comes from the real-life experiences of thousands of small business owners, financial advisors included, most of whom were hopelessly confused about money when I met them. Once they understood and accepted the following principles, they developed a clarity about money that could only be called enlightened.

The First Kind of Money: Income

Income is the money financial advisors are paid by their practice for doing their job *in* the practice. It's what they get paid for going to work every day.

Clearly, if financial advisors didn't do their job, others would have to, and *they* would be paid the money the practice currently pays the financial advisors. Income, then, has nothing to do with *ownership*. Income is solely the province of *employee-ship*.

That's why to the financial advisor-as-*employee*, income is the most important form money can take. To the financial advisor-as-*owner*, however, it is the least important form money can take.

Most important; least important. Do you see the conflict? The conflict between the financial advisor-as-employee and the financial advisor-as-owner?

We'll deal with this conflict later. For now, just know that it is potentially the most paralyzing conflict in a financial advisor's life.

Failing to resolve this conflict will cripple you. Resolving it will set you free.

The Second Kind of Money: Profit

Profit is what's left over after a financial advisory practice has done its job effectively and efficiently. If there is no profit, the practice is doing something wrong.

However, just because the practice shows a profit does not mean it is necessarily doing all the right things in the right way. Instead, it just means that something was done right during or preceding the period in which the profit was earned.

The important issue here is whether the profit was intentional or accidental. If it happened by accident (which most profit does), don't take credit for it. You'll live to regret your impertinence.

If it happened intentionally, take all the credit you want. You've earned it. Because profit created intentionally, rather than by accident, is replicable—again and again. And your practice's ability to repeat its performance is the most critical ability it can have.

As you'll soon see, the value of money is a function of your practice's ability to produce it in predictable amounts at an above-average return on investment.

Profit can be understood only in the context of your practice's purpose, as opposed to *your* purpose as a financial advisor. Profit, then, fuels the forward motion of the practice that produces it. This is accomplished in four ways:

- Profit is *investment capital* that feeds and supports growth.
- Profit is *bonus capital* that rewards people for exceptional work.
- Profit is *operating capital* that shores up money shortfalls.
- Profit is *return-on-investment* capital that rewards you, the financial advisor-owner, for taking risks.

Without profit, a financial advisory practice cannot subsist, much less grow. Profit is the fuel of progress.

If a practice misuses or abuses profit, however, the penalty is much like having no profit at all. Imagine the plight of a financial advisor who has way too much return-on-investment capital and not enough investment capital, bonus capital, and operating capital. Can you see the imbalance this creates?

The Third Kind of Money: Flow

Flow is what money *does* in a financial advisory practice, as opposed to what money *is*. Whether the practice is large or small, money tends to move erratically through it, much like a pinball. One minute it's there; the next minute it's not.

Flow can be even more critical to a practice's survival than profit, because a practice can produce a profit and still be short of money. Has this ever happened to you? It's called profit on paper rather than in fact.

No matter how large your practice, if the money isn't there when it's needed, you're threatened—regardless of how much profit you've made. You can borrow it, of course. But money acquired in dire circumstances is almost always the most expensive kind of money you can get.

Knowing where the money is and where it will be when you need it is a critically important task of both the financial advisor-as-employee and the financial advisor-as-owner.

Rules of Flow

You will learn no more important lesson than the huge impact flow can have on the health and survival of your financial advisory practice, let alone your business or enterprise. The following two rules will help you understand why this subject is so critical.

1. The First Rule of Flow states that your income statement
   is static, while the flow is dynamic. Your income statement
   is a snapshot, while the flow is a moving picture. So, while
   your income statement is an excellent tool for analyzing
   your practice *after* the fact, it's a poor tool for managing it
   in the heat of the moment.

Your income statement tells you (1) how much money you're spending and where, and (2) how much money you're receiving and from where.

Flow gives you the same information as the income statement, plus it tells you *when* you're spending and receiving money. In other words, flow is an income statement moving through time. And that is the key to understanding flow. It is about management in real time. How much is coming in? How much is going out? You'd like to know this daily, or even by the hour if possible. Never by the week or month.

You must be able to forecast flow. You must have a flow plan that helps you gain a clear vision of the money that's out there next month and the month after that. You must also pinpoint what your needs will be in the future.

Ultimately, however, when it comes to flow, the action is always in the moment. It's about *now*. The minute you start to meander away from the present, you'll miss the boat.

Unfortunately, few financial advisors pay any attention to flow until it dries up completely and slow pay becomes no pay. They are oblivious to this kind of detail until, say, clients announce that they won't pay for this or that. That gets a financial advisor's attention because the expenses keep on coming.

When it comes to flow, most financial advisors are flying by the proverbial seat of their pants. No matter how many people you hire to take care of your money, until you change the way you think about it, you will always be out of luck. No one can do this for you.

Managing flow takes attention to detail. But when flow is managed, your life takes on an incredible sheen. You're swimming with the current, not against it. You're in charge!

2. The Second Rule of Flow states that money seldom moves as you expect it to. But you do have the power to change that, provided you understand the two primary sources of money as it comes in and goes out of your financial advisory practice.

The truth is, the more control you have over the *source* of money, the more control you have over its flow. The sources of money are both inside and outside your practice.

Money comes from *outside* your practice in the form of receivables, reimbursements, investments, and loans.

Money comes from *inside* your practice in the form of payables, taxes, capital investments, and payroll. These are the costs associated with attracting clients, delivering your services, operations, and so forth.

Few financial advisors see the money going *out* of their practice as a source of money, but it is.

When considering how to spend money in your practice, you can save—and therefore make—money in three ways:

- Do it more effectively.
- Do it more efficiently.
- Stop doing it altogether.

By identifying the money sources inside and outside your practice, and then applying these methods, you will be immeasurably better at controlling the flow in your practice.

But what are these sources? They include how you

- manage your services;
- buy supplies and equipment;
- compensate your people;
- plan people's use of time;
- determine the direct cost of your services;
- increase the number of clients seen;
- manage your work;
- collect reimbursements and receivables; and
- countless more.

In fact, every task performed in your practice (and ones you haven't yet learned how to perform) can be done more efficiently and effectively, dramatically reducing the cost of doing business. In the process, you will create more income, produce more profit, and balance the flow.

The Fourth Kind of Money: Equity

Sadly, few financial advisors fully appreciate the value of equity in their financial advisory practice. Yet, equity is the second most valuable asset any financial advisor will ever possess. (The first most valuable asset is, of course, your life. More on that later.)

Equity is the financial value placed on your financial advisory practice by a prospective buyer.

Thus, your *practice* is your most important product, not your services. Because your practice has the power to set you free. That's right. Once you sell your practice—providing you get what you want for it—you're free!

Of course, to enhance your equity, to increase your practice's value, you have to build it right. You have to build a practice that works. A practice that can become a true business and a business that can become a true enterprise. A practice/business/enterprise that can produce income, profit, flow, and equity better than any other financial advisor's practice can.

To accomplish that, your practice must be designed so that it can do what it does systematically and predictably, every single time.

The Story of McDonald's

Let me tell you the most unlikely story anyone has ever told you about the successful building of a financial advisory practice, business, and enterprise. Let me tell you the story of Ray Kroc.

You might be thinking, "What on earth does a hamburger stand have to do with my practice? I'm not in the hamburger business; I'm a financial advisor."

Yes, you are. But by practicing financial advisory services as you have been taught, you've abandoned any chance to expand your reach, help more clients, or improve your services the way they must be improved if the practice of financial advisory services—and your life—is going to be transformed.

In Kroc's story lies the answer.

Kroc called his first McDonald's restaurant "a little money machine." That's why thousands of franchisees bought it. And the reason it worked? Kroc demanded consistency, so that a hamburger in Philadelphia would be an advertisement for one in Peoria. In fact, no matter where you bought a McDonald's hamburger in the 1950s, the meat patty was guaranteed to weigh exactly 1.6 ounces, with a diameter of $3^5/8$ inches. It was in the McDonald's Operation Manual.

Did Kroc succeed? You know he did! And so can you, once you understand his methods. Consider just one part of his story.

In 1954, Kroc made his living selling the five-spindle Multimixer milkshake machine. He heard about a hamburger stand in San Bernardino, California, that had eight of his machines in operation, meaning it could make forty shakes simultaneously. This he had to see.

Kroc flew from Chicago to Los Angeles, then drove sixty miles to San Bernardino. As he sat in his car outside Mac and Dick McDonald's restaurant, he watched as lunch customers lined up for bags of hamburgers.

In a revealing moment, Kroc approached a strawberry blonde in a yellow convertible. As he later described it, "It was not her sex appeal but the obvious relish with which she devoured the hamburger that made my pulse begin to hammer with excitement."

Passion.

In fact, it was the french fry that truly captured his heart. Before the 1950s, it was almost impossible to buy fries of consistent quality. Kroc changed all that. "The french fry," he once wrote, "would become almost sacrosanct for me, its preparation a ritual to be followed religiously."

Passion and preparation.

The potatoes had to be just so—top-quality Idaho russets, eight ounces apiece, deep-fried to a golden brown, and salted with a shaker that, as Kroc put it, kept going "like a Salvation Army girl's tambourine."

As Kroc soon learned, potatoes too high in water content—and even top-quality Idaho russets varied greatly in water content— will come out soggy when fried. And so Kroc sent out teams of workers, armed with hydrometers, to make sure all his suppliers were producing potatoes in the optimal solids range of 20 to 23 percent.

Preparation and passion. Passion and preparation. Look those words up in the dictionary and you'll see Kroc's picture. Can you envision your picture there?

Do you understand what Kroc did? Do you see why he was able to sell thousands of franchises? Kroc knew the true value of equity, and unlike Steve from our story, Kroc went to work *on* his business rather than *in* his business. He knew the hamburger wasn't his product—McDonald's was!

So what does *your* financial advisory practice need to do to become a little money machine? What is the passion that will drive you to build a practice that works—a turnkey system like Ray Kroc's?

Equity and the Turnkey System

What's a turnkey system? And why is it so valuable to you? To better understand it, let's look at another example of a turnkey system that worked to perfection: the recordings of Frank Sinatra.

Frank Sinatra's records were to him as McDonald's restaurants were to Ray Kroc. They were part of a turnkey system that allowed Sinatra to sing to millions of people without having to be there himself.

Sinatra's recordings were a dependable turnkey system that worked predictably, systematically, automatically, and effortlessly to produce the same results every single time—no matter where they were played, and no matter who was listening.

Regardless of where Sinatra was, his records just kept on producing income, profit, flow, and equity, over and over . . . and still do! Sinatra needed only to produce the prototype recording, and the system did the rest.

Kroc's McDonald's is another prototypical turnkey solution, addressing everything McDonald's needs to do in a basic, systematic way so that anyone properly trained by McDonald's can successfully reproduce the same results.

And this is where you'll realize your equity opportunity: in the way your practice does business; in the way your practice systematically does what you intend it to do; and in the development of your turnkey system—a system that works even in the hands of ordinary people (and financial advisors less experienced than you) to produce extraordinary results.

Remember:

- If you want to build vast equity in your practice, then go to work *on* your practice, building it into a business that works every single time.

- Go to work *on* your practice to build a totally integrated turnkey system that delivers exactly what you promised every single time.

- Go to work *on* your practice to package it and make it stand out from the financial advisory practices you see everywhere else.

Here is the most important idea you will ever hear about your practice and what it can potentially provide for you:

The value of your equity is directly proportional to how well your practice works. And how well your practice works is directly proportional to the effectiveness of the systems you have put into place upon which the operation of your practice depends.

Whether money takes the form of income, profit, flow, or equity, the amount of it—and how much of it stays with you—invariably boils down to this. Money, happiness, life—it all depends on how well your practice works. Not on your people, not on you, but on the system.

Your practice holds the secret to more money. Are you ready to learn how to find it?

Earlier in this chapter, I alerted you to the inevitable conflict between the financial advisor-as-employee and the financial advisor-as-owner. It's a battle between the part of you working *in* the practice and the part of you working *on* the practice. Between the part of you working for income and the part of you working for equity.

Here's how to resolve this conflict:

1. Be honest with yourself about whether you're filling *employee* shoes or *owner* shoes.

2. As your practice's key employee, determine the most effective way to do the job you're doing, *and then document that job.*

3. Once you've documented the job, create a strategy for replacing yourself with someone else (another financial advisor) who will then use your documented system exactly as you do.

4. Have your new employees manage the newly delegated system. Improve the system by quantifying its effectiveness over time.

5. Repeat this process throughout your practice wherever you catch yourself acting as employee rather than owner.

6. Learn to distinguish between ownership work and employee-ship work every step of the way.

Master these methods, understand the difference between the four kinds of money, develop an interest in how money works in your practice . . . and then watch it flow in with the speed and efficiency of a perfectly delivered golf swing.

Now let's take another step in our strategic thinking process. Let's look at the subject of *planning*. But first, let's listen to what Michael Steranka has to say about money. ✤

Money Dynamics – Seeing is Believing

Michael Steranka

Money is usually attracted, not pursued.

—Jim Rohn

Money? You might look at the title of this chapter and think you've got this down pat. You're a financial advisor, after all. You advise other people about money for a living.

But the reality is that financial advisors find money . . . confusing.

Although many advisors know how to counsel other individuals or corporations about their finances, they don't have a clue about managing the money in their own firm. Yes, it sounds ridiculous to say that out loud. But I assure you that it's not just you.

In this chapter, you will begin to take ownership of the map to success by identifying your first roadblock: money. You know what money means within the services you offer. But what does money look like in the context of the business of financial services?

If you're like most financial advisors, you didn't start your business because you have a knack for choosing rent space and

31

hiring employees. In fact, those duties were probably the last things on your mind.

Before launching their businesses, most planners have their eyes set on the greener grass on the other side of the fence. In a stroke of supposed genius, they think, *I'm going to go out and start my own firm!* Then when they do, every thought turns into, *What the hell am I doing here?* These planners haven't the slightest idea about what they're doing.

If you identify with them—and at one point, we've all identified with them—then you need to figure out what to do with money. Otherwise, you won't make it.

We all want money. But when we get it, we don't know what to do with it. We always think the good times will always be good. But in that same vein, when we have bad times, we fear they will never end.

What you need is a plan. You need to understand the long-term effects of the money you spend today. Unless you can recognize how every dollar spent affects your business, you will wind up with no business at all.

All right. We admit that money in this context is something we never wanted to deal with. So what should we do with all that money?

Before we talk about what needs to be done with our money, let's talk about what financial advisors have been doing wrong with money.

What do most advisors do when they want to make more money? They work longer hours. They work and work until their family wonders what they're doing and begin to ask questions like, "Are you nuts?"

The E-Myth answer is to work smarter, not harder. Work *on* your business, not *in* your business. The solution to making more money isn't to multiply whatever strategy you're using now. If you've got the wrong strategy, then twice as much work won't equal twice as much money.

The solution is to restrategize. Pick a new game plan.

Michael E. Gerber's E-Myth philosophy says that being a good carpenter has no bearing on running a good carpentry business. I could build a fabulous bookcase, but I might not know the first thing about constructing a good payroll or placing an ad in the *Yellow Pages*. This applies to financial advisors, as well. You might be the greatest financial advisor ever to exist, but unless you know how to be a great businessperson, your business will always fall short of your expectations.

Financial advisors receive so much training about what to do with a client *after* they get that client. But who can tell you how to set up your business or how to run it?

How do you know how to make payroll? Or how to hire people and fire people? Do you know how to negotiate the rent on your office space? What about the rent on equipment? What kind of marketing campaigns are the most efficient? What about public relations? Continuing education?

If you're serious about this journey, then you have to ask for directions.

I suggest that you approach the people who have survived these experiences. Interview them and ask for their counsel. Ask, "What do I do? What's the best way to do it? How do I grow my business?" We'll touch on growth in later chapters, but the point I'm making is that although you might understand how a 401(k) should be allocated and how much money people need to save, it takes an entirely different mindset to figure out what you need to spend.

The first question you should ask yourself is, "What is my budget for running my own company?"

If you're just starting out, how can you be realistic with yourself? Do you set sky-high projections that you know are not doable? Or do you aim low to avoid failure so you never take any chances to grow and never spend any money? Frankly, the right answer is somewhere between those two.

I ask myself question after question regarding income. The temptation may be to avoid these topics altogether, but trust me, the more time you spend analyzing the monetary trends associated with your business, the more peace of mind you will have.

Start by asking these questions: How much money do I want to earn? How many clients do I need in order to make the income that

I want? What is the average revenue per client, per year, over the lifetime of the client?

Ask these questions over and over again throughout the course of the year. Sometimes, I ask myself a few of my questions in different intervals throughout the day, let alone the year.

I'm a big yellow notepad guy. I have a hundred yellow notepads everywhere, and I need to have my notes and crazy graphs. At least fifty times a year, I go through my numbers just to make sure that I'll get through the next month. Even though I have a system, I want to write everything down, visualize my goals, and make sure they're realistic.

As you're thinking about money, direct your thoughts to profit. The journey of a thousand miles begins with the first step, and the first step comes from profit.

Gross is nice, but net is better. You can gross a huge amount, but what matters is how much you get to keep.

In order to understand profit, you have to have a formula separate from a quick glance at your *QuickBooks* spreadsheets. Profit is the glue that will keep your company secure. Mismanage profit, take it for granted, or misjudge it and that profit will disappear in the blink of an eye. Like time, profit cannot be recovered.

On the other hand, if profit is properly nurtured, it can ensure that all your dreams come true. When I say "dreams," I'm not only talking about money, but also referring to other areas of your life. Growing and learning with your business will change you holistically. Even my spiritual life has improved because of the discipline I've acquired while learning to run a financial advisory firm successfully. My family life has improved as well. Even the time that I can spend volunteering in my community has grown as a result of my business. We will touch on this kind of growth in later chapters.

Unfortunately, 70 percent of the dozens of financial advisors I have shared my story with haven't been able to tell me with certainty what their profit was, what their profit is, or even what their profit should be.

Then when I make a suggestion, the financial advisor I'm talking to would shut down and say, "I can't do that." "I'm different." "It's different in the Midwest . . . or in the West . . . or in the city." "My market is different." One financial advisor would tell me, "I deal with people who have less money than your clients," while another would say, "I deal with people who have more money than your clients."

People with that mentality—people who believe that "this works for you, but could never work for me" and can't shake that lie—are people destined for mediocrity.

With everything financial advisors have to deal with in this industry, I believe that we should be well compensated. Too many financial advisors claim to be happy with $50,000 a year. Frankly, I'm not satisfied with $50,000 a week. It's all about shifting your perspective. Aim high.

Now let's get practical and translate these ideas to formulas.

How do you find out how much you need to make in order to maintain a certain amount of profit? Begin by figuring out what you want your annual profit to be. Then break that number down to your quarterly profit, then your monthly amount, then your daily amount.

Let's play with some numbers. Let's say you need $250,000 gross to meet your profit goal of $125,000. Let's then say that you average 5 percent in compensation on the money that you bring to your firm. That money can be a combination of managed accounts, annuity premiums, mutual funds, life insurance, long-term care, disability, and health insurance.

If 5 percent of the net assets you bring amounts to $250,000, then you need to bring in $5 million each year.

Now that you know how much you want to bring in, you have to figure out what kind of vacation time you want with your family. Then you gauge how much time you'd like to spend learning to work *on* your business and not *in* it. So you take six weeks off for those needs out of the fifty-two weeks in a year, and are left with forty-six weeks.

Then you realize that you want your weekends to yourself. You want to remember what it's like to have a five day workweek. So you have forty-six weeks at five days a week of work, which is two hundred thirty days. Now you need to take into consideration other holidays or days when the market is closed. You figure out there are eleven of those days, so that leaves you with a total of 219 total work-days per year.

If you take the $5 million and divide it by 219 days, you will find that you need to bring in approximately $22,831 in new business each day.

The next step is to figure out what financial products or services that help your clients reach their goals will generate $22,831 each day. You could put a large chunk in mutual funds, or explore more life insurance premiums or annuities. You get the idea.

The imperative thing is to apply this formula to your goals. Break down your numbers until you find your daily goal. If you have a better understanding of how much you need each day to make it work, then you will have better control over making that happen.

If you write down your goal as simply being $5 million of new assets under management in a year, it will seem daunting and you'll give up the day after you make your resolution! But $23,000 a day sounds much more feasible. That's something you can get excited about and actually work toward—and that's only 219 days out of the year!

Now you have a starting point from which you can start to think about your money. You know exactly what you need to bring in each day and you can even take a guilt-free vacation. You can spend time volunteering, pick up a hobby, or work out and stay in shape. You can learn more about your business and become an expert in a niche market. You can reacquaint yourself with your children and your spouse.

Now that you have a better sense of how much money needs to come in and at what rate, let's talk about how much money needs to go out.

Financial advisors cringe when they hear that dreadful word, *flow*.

Flow refers to the movement of money in and out of your bank account. Flow is as essential to the life of a business as air is to the human race. You might think I'm joking, but I've seen too many practices fail, or seen their owners be forced to sell out or suffer involuntary retirement.

In order to understand flow, you need to be aware of how and when you receive compensation. When are fees deducted and when do they hit your account? When are commissions deducted and when do they hit your account? If you do seminars, what are seasonal trends like?

You have to pay attention to things like rent and payroll, information technology (IT), and staffing needs. This can change depending on if you're busier around tax time or at end of the year.

You'll need at least two to three years of data to start analyzing trends. But once you start analyzing, patterns will emerge and you will see your business with a fresh set of eyes. You will feel empowered. You'll never be caught flatfooted again.

Next, you need to establish a solid banking relationship. Granted, the banking world has changed greatly and your contacts may have jumped ship to stronger banks, but go with them. Those banking relationships can be essential to your planning.

Remember that banks love organization, which means that when you can show them that you have your financial house in order, they will be much more inclined to extend a helping hand. And take advantage of that helping hand *before* you need it. Get a line of credit and use it, if needed. Sometimes I used my credit even when I didn't need it just to show the bank that I appreciated it. As you deal with banks and have a better idea of the power of income, profit, and flow, you will be rewarded with equity.

Ah, sweet equity! Don't confuse *sweet* equity with *sweat* equity, which is what it used to be before you picked up this book! Now you're on your way to a real business with real value, and that's simply sweet.

When that business value is recognized in the marketplace, you can sell your business because of the economic prosperity it could afford someone else. Then you will have reached your payday—perhaps the biggest payday of your life!

When you reach this point, you have something close to what Michael E. Gerber calls "The Turnkey System." You've unlocked the value of all the hours, days, weeks, months, and years you invested into your constant systematizing.

Now you have the ability to take your show on the road, sell it, or keep it and let it send checks to your account on a daily or weekly basis. Michael E. Gerber is absolutely on point when he says that this is the reason to enter the business world. If not this, then why not just work for someone else your entire career and place your fate and that of your family in someone else's hands? No thanks!

You're building a business with an exit strategy in mind. You might work on that business your entire life, but the beauty behind the E-Myth is that you can reach a point where you don't have to. You'll keep going only if you want to.

How would you feel knowing you are creating such a financial advisory firm? Would you be passionate about it? Would that passion show when talking to clients or prospective clients? You bet! And what's the result of that passion? More success. What a concept.

To go about all of this correctly, you can't stop growing. Make it a point to constantly improve yourself and your business.

Make a list of thirty-six potential areas of improvement. List them in order of importance and focus on adopting three improvements each month.

When you check your list in three to six months, you'll find that many of the items near the bottom of your list have self-corrected because of the changes you have implemented. I have seen this self-correcting pattern repeated over the years in my own financial advisory firm.

If you're at a loss for where to start, I recommend these three things for the top of your list:

- Get an extra hour of sleep every night.
- Eat better.
- Work out for an hour a day, four days a week.

I once attended a high-powered coaching seminar during which every businessperson in the room was told to get an extra hour of sleep every night for the next ninety days. The number of success stories that came from just that one lifestyle improvement was astounding.

Remember that even in the face of those thirty-six areas of improvement, everything takes time and diligent effort. Rome was not built in a day and neither will your financial advisory firm be built in a day.

However, the E-Myth provides a clear roadmap to success, and most of all, it gives us hope. It reminds us that there's no such thing as a "pipe dream." The E-Myth provides the inspiration and guidance we need to turn our dreams to reality. It puts the wind in your sails. Next, read on to see what Michael E. Gerber has to say about planning. ✤

CHAPTER 5

On the Subject of Planning

Michael E. Gerber

Luck is good planning, carefully executed.

—Anonymous

A nother obvious oversight revealed in Steve and Peggy's story was the absence of true planning.

Every financial advisor starting his or her own practice must have a plan. You should never begin to see clients without a plan in place. But, like Steve, most financial advisors do exactly that.

A financial advisor lacking a vision is simply someone who goes to work every day. Someone who is just doing it, doing it, doing it. Busy, busy, busy. Maybe making money, maybe not. Maybe getting something out of life, maybe not. Taking chances without really taking control.

The plan tells anyone who needs to know *how we do things here.* The plan defines the objective and the process by which you will attain it. The plan encourages you to organize tasks into functions, and then helps people grasp the logic of each of those functions. This in turn permits you to bring new employees up to speed quickly.

There are numerous books and seminars on the subject of practice management, but they focus on making you a better financial advisor. I want to teach you something else that you've never been taught before: how to be a manager. It has nothing to do with conventional practice management and everything to do with thinking like an entrepreneur.

The Planning Triangle

As we discussed in the preface, every financial advisory practice is a company, every financial advisory business is a company, and every financial advisory enterprise is a company. Yet the difference between the three is extraordinary. Although all three may offer financial advisory services, how they do what they do is completely different.

The trouble with most companies owned by financial advisors is that they are dependent on the financial advisor. That's because they're a practice—the smallest, most limited form a company can take. Practices are formed around the technician, whether financial advisor or roofer.

You may choose in the beginning to form a practice, but you should understand its limitations. The company called a *practice* depends on the owner—that is, the financial advisor. The company called a *business* depends on other people plus a system by which that business does what it does. Once your practice becomes a business, you can replicate it, turning it into an *enterprise*.

Consider the example of Sea Financial Services. The clients don't come in asking Douglas Sea, although he is one of the top financial advisors around. After all, he can only handle so many cases a day and be in only one location at a time.

Yet he wants to offer his high-quality services to more people in the community. If he has reliable systems in place—systems that any qualified associate financial advisor can learn to use—he has created a business and it can be replicated. Douglas can then go on to offer his services—which demand his guidance, not his presence—in a multitude of different settings. He can open dozens of financial advisory practices, none of which need Douglas himself, except in the role of entrepreneur.

Is your financial advisory company going to be a practice, a business, or an enterprise? Planning is crucial to answering this all-important question. Whatever you choose to do must be communicated by your plan, which is really three interrelated plans in one. We call it the Planning Triangle, and it consists of the following:

- The business plan
- The practice plan
- The completion plan

The three plans form a triangle, with the business plan at the base, the practice plan in the center, and the completion plan at the apex:

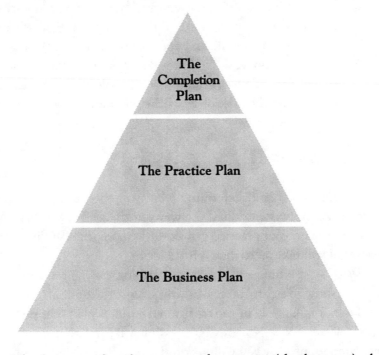

The business plan determines *who* you are (the business), the practice plan determines *what* you do (the specific focus of your financial advisory practice), and the completion plan determines *how* you do it (the fulfillment process).

By looking at the Planning Triangle, we see that the three critical plans are interconnected. The connection between them is established by asking the following questions:

1. Who are we?
2. What do we do?
3. How do we do it?

Who are we? is purely a strategic question.
What do we do? is both a strategic and a tactical question.
How do we do it? is both a strategic and a tactical question.

Strategic questions shape the vision and destiny of your business, of which your practice is only one essential component. Tactical questions turn that vision into reality. Thus, strategic questions provide the foundation for tactical questions, just as the base provides the foundation for the middle and apex of your Planning Triangle.

First ask: What do we do and how do we do it . . . *strategically?*
And then: What do we do and how do we do it . . . *practically?*
Let's look at how the three plans will help you develop your practice.

The Business Plan

Your business plan will determine what you choose to do in your financial advisory practice and the way you choose to do it. Without a business plan, your practice can do little more than survive. And even that will take more than a little luck.

Without a business plan, you're treading water in a deep pool with no shore in sight. You're working against the natural flow.

I'm not talking about the traditional business plan that is taught in business schools. No, this business plan reads like a story—the most important story you will ever tell.

Your business plan must clearly describe

- the business you are creating;
- the purpose it will serve;

- the vision it will pursue;
- the process through which you will turn that vision into a reality; and
- the way money will be used to realize your vision.

Build your business plan with *business* language, not *practice* language (the language of the financial advisor). Make sure the plan focuses on matters of interest to your lenders and shareholders rather than just your technicians. It should rely on demographics and psychographics to tell you who buys and why; it should also include projections for return on investment and return on equity. Use it to detail both the market and the strategy through which you intend to become a leader in that market, not as a financial advisor but as a business enterprise.

The business plan, though absolutely essential, is only one of three critical plans every financial advisor needs to create and implement. Now let's take a look at the practice plan.

The Practice Plan

The practice plan includes everything a financial advisor needs to know, have, and do in order to deliver his or her promise to a client on time, every time.

Every task should prompt you to ask three questions:

1. What do I need to know?
2. What do I need to have?
3. What do I need to do?

What Do I Need to *Know?*

What information do I need to satisfy my promise on time, every time, exactly as promised? In order to recognize what you need to know, you must understand the expectations of others, including your clients, your associates, and other employees. Are you clear on those expectations? Don't make the mistake of assuming you know. Instead, create a need-to-know checklist to make sure you ask all the necessary questions.

A need-to-know checklist might look like this:

- What are the expectations of my clients?
- What are the expectations of my administrators?
- What are the expectations of my associate financial advisors?
- What are the expectations of my staff?

What Do I Need to *Have*?

This question raises the issue of resources—namely, money, people, and time. If you don't have enough money to finance operations, how can you fulfill those expectations without creating cash-flow problems? If you don't have enough trained people, what happens then? And if you don't have enough time to manage your practice, what happens when you can't be in two places at once?

Don't assume that you can get what you need when you need it. Most often, you can't. And even if you can get what you need at the last minute, you'll pay dearly for it.

What Do I Need to *Do*?

The focus here is on actions to be started and finished. What do I need to do to fulfill the expectations of this client on time, every time, exactly as promised? For example, what exactly are the steps to perform when seeing someone with financial problems and related investment issues, or when designing the right retirement investment plan?

Your clients fall into distinct categories, and those categories make up your practice. The best financial advisory practices will invariably focus on fewer and fewer categories as they discover the importance of doing one thing better than anyone else.

Answering the question *What do I need to do?* demands a series of action plans, including:

- the objective to be achieved;
- the standards by which you will know that the objective has been achieved;
- the benchmarks you need to reach in order for the objective to be achieved;
- the function/person accountable for the completion of the benchmarks;
- the budget for the completion of each benchmark; and
- the time by which each benchmark must be completed.

Your action plans should become the foundation for the completion plans. And the reason you need completion plans is to ensure that everything you do is not only realistic but can also be managed.

The Completion Plan

If the practice plan gives you results and provides you with standards, the completion plan tells you everything you need to know about every benchmark in the practice plan—that is, how you're going to fulfill client expectations on time, every time, as promised. In other words, how you're going to arrange a referral to another professional, make routine adjustments to a client's portfolio, update a client's income for a life plan, or help a client decide whether to apply for life insurance or long-term care.

The completion plan is essentially the operations manual, providing information about the details of doing tactical work. It is a guide to tell the people responsible for doing that work exactly how to do it.

Every completion plan becomes a part of the knowledge base of your business. No completion plan goes to waste. Every completion plan becomes a kind of textbook that explains to new employees or new associates joining your team how your practice operates in a way that distinguishes it from all other financial advisory practices.

To return to an earlier example, the completion plan for making a Big Mac is explicitly described in the *McDonald's Operation Manual,* as is every completion plan needed to run a McDonald's business.

The completion plan for a financial advisor might include the step-by-step details of how to analyze where the client is now with both the size of his estate and current asset allocation—in contrast to how everyone else has learned to do it. Of course, all those who work in financial advisory services have done this analysis. They've learned to do it the same way everyone else has learned to do it. But if you are going to stand out as unique in the minds of your clients, employees, and others, you must invent your own way of doing even ordinary things. Most of that value-added perception will come from your communication skills, your listening skills, and your innovative skills into transforming an ordinary visit into a client experience.

Perhaps you'll decide that a mandatory part of your service offer is to map out the clients' income for the rest of their life. Factoring in life expectancy and whether they have guaranteed sources of income in retirement, you may discuss the survivorship of said plans to the appropriate beneficiaries. Help the clients to understand how much risk they are actually taking if the equity markets do not cooperate and if there is a health incident. Most clients may have never had this special treatment until now. If no other financial advisor your client has seen has ever taken the time to explain the process, you'll immediately set yourself apart. You must constantly raise the questions, *How do we do it here? How should we do it here?*

The quality of your answers will determine how effectively you distinguish your practice from every other financial advisor's practice.

Benchmarks

You can measure the movement of your practice—from what it is today to what it will be in the future—using business benchmarks. These are the goals you want your business to achieve during its lifetime.

Your benchmarks should include the following:

- Financial benchmarks
- Emotional benchmarks (the impact your practice will have on everyone who comes into contact with it)
- Performance benchmarks
- Client benchmarks (Who are they? Why do they come to you? What will your practice give them that no one else will?)
- Employee benchmarks (How do you grow people? How do you find people who want to grow? How do you create a school in your practice that will teach your people skills they can't learn anywhere else?)

Your business benchmarks will reflect (1) the position your practice will hold in the minds and hearts of your clients, employees, and investors; and (2) how you intend to make that position a reality through the systems you develop.

Your benchmarks will describe how your management team will take shape and what systems you will need to develop so that your managers, just like McDonald's managers, will be able to produce the results for which they will be held accountable.

Benefits of the Planning Triangle

By implementing the Planning Triangle, you will discover

- what your practice will look, act, and feel like when it's fully evolved;
- when that's going to happen;

- how much money you will make; and
- much more.

These, then, are the primary purposes of the three critical plans: (1) to clarify precisely what needs to be done to get what the financial advisor wants from his or her practice and life, and (2) to define the specific steps by which it will happen.

First *this* must happen, then *that* must happen. One, two, three. By monitoring your progress, step by step, you can determine whether you're on the right track.

That's what planning is all about. It's about creating a standard—a yardstick—against which you will be able to measure your performance.

Failing to create such a standard is like throwing a straw into a hurricane. Who knows where that straw will land?

Have you taken the leap? Have you accepted that the word *business* and the word *practice* are not synonymous? That a practice relies on the financial advisor and a business relies on other people plus a system?

Because most financial advisors are control freaks, 99 percent of today's financial advisory companies are practices, not businesses.

The result, as a friend of mine says, is that "financial advisors are spending all day stamping out fires when all around them the forest is ablaze. They're out of touch, and that financial advisor better take control of the practice before someone else does."

Because financial advisors are never taught to think like entrepreneurs, the bureaucratic system is forever at war with the entrepreneur. This is especially evident in large, multidisciplinary practices, where bureaucrats (corporate management) often try to control financial advisors (entrepreneurs). They usually end up treating each other as combatants. In fact, the single greatest reason financial advisors become entrepreneurs is to divorce such bureaucrats and to begin to reinvent the financial advisory enterprise.

That's you. Now the divorce is over and a new love affair has begun. You're a financial advisor with a plan! Who wouldn't want to do business with such a person?

Now let's take the next step in our strategic odyssey. Let's take a closer look at the subject of *management*. But before we do, let's listen to what Michael Steranka has to say about planning. ✤

> To find out exactly what your three critical plans will look like when they're finished, go to www.michaelegerber.com/co-author.

6

Planning
Your Course

Michael Steranka

If it gets out of the harbor at all, it will either sink, or wind up on some deserted beach, a derelict.

—Earl Nightingale

A ship with missing parts—broken rudder, a missing helm, or even an incomplete crew—will not reach its destination. To ensure you have a successful business, your ship needs all of its necessary parts. To keep track of all those parts, you need to plan.

I read a survey of CEOs a few years ago that revealed the average CEO spends nearly 35 percent of his or her time in strategic planning. That's a high percentage, but it's credible and shows the value of careful and deliberate planning for growth. This is the freedom that an E-Myth-driven business can provide. Do you want to experience the freedom that results from a vision that has taken hold so well that your company can operate even without you? This chapter will show you that this freedom is a direct result of planning.

So what is "planning?" Planning is dreaming big. Imagining. Creating. Ask yourself, "What relationships do I want? How can they further my career? How can I think bigger? Think differently?"

Planning means offering yourself to anything—such as a film, a crossword puzzle, or a video game—that makes you think outside the box. I recently attended a conference where the speaker was a man born with no arms. This man is a professional golfer and tennis instructor, which shows you that nothing is impossible. And when you begin to plan as though nothing really is impossible, doors open where you once saw walls.

If you don't have a giant team of people working for you, allocating 35 percent of your time to planning probably isn't feasible. So devote 10 percent of your time to strategic planning, and then push yourself to step it up by 5 percent a year. I found that utilizing the benefits of a coach/mentor will usually allow a person to maximize the time spent on strategic planning. Let's face it, you don't have any time to just waste.

In the beginning stages of your business, there is also the danger of too much future prospecting. An art form is picking up money today. Keep doing what you're doing, but don't forget what's paying your bills right now. Gradually ease new practices into your business, but if those practices are as good as people say they are, they'll be good three months, six months, or a year from now.

As you begin planning, imagine the life you'd live if you were to make a certain amount of money each month. Say you're starting out and you'd like to make $10,000 a month. Write down twenty things you would do with that $10,000. Then consider, what kind of car would you drive? Would your personal relationships change? Where would you vacation? Would you travel? What kind of gifts would you buy your spouse? How would you spoil your kids? Would you give the money to a church? I've made this list five or six times throughout my career, and when I look back at my early writings, I think, *Holy smokes, I was really thinking small!*

Writing down the thing I want to achieve—such as losing weight, eating better, or improving my relationship with my family—helps the goal take leaps toward reality. Success starts taking shape the moment we write down our goals and think about them.

Planning is a survival skill. It's being realistic when looking at your gross income, and then factoring in your salary, payroll, marketing costs, office rent, and other expenses. Some people never make it because they don't plan. They guess. Sometimes they guess right and sometimes they guess wrong, but "eyeballing" matters of money oftentimes means checking the bank account at the end of the year to find nothing there.

As Michael E. Gerber mentioned in the previous chapter, planning is comprised of a triangle with three points: *the business plan, the practice plan,* and *the completion plan.*

The business plan reads like a story, and it's the most important story you will ever tell. It defines who you are and what you're creating. Instead of using industry jargon, use a universal business language to help others understand your vision. Explain your dream from scratch. Answer questions such as, "Why did I choose this business?" Then make a few projections for returns on investment and returns on equity for your company. But be realistic. Remember that this is your starting point; it isn't the end game.

The practice plan, or the "what we do" element, goes into specifics. Even if you don't know what those specifics are, you'll find that they'll come to you as you work through this point. Ask "how" questions, as in: "How do I get clients, retain clients, and keep clients happy?" "What market am I targeting and how do I reach it?" "How do I make sure my office location allows easy access to clients?" "How many employees do I need now? How many will I need in the future?"

As you expand, consider what additional services you'd like to make available to your clients. Anticipate increasing staffing needs and additional office space or technology needs. Factor in higher marketing expenses. Mapping out these plans will untangle the visions you have for your business, which will translate to a confidence that even your clients and prospective clients will notice.

The completion plan is the secret sauce—the formation of your systems manual. In the manual, define everything you do, how you do it, how you measure it, and how you monitor it. Being this comprehensive is time-consuming, but it is also the most fun and liberating part of the process.

The completion plan covers everything from turning the lights on in the morning to shutting them off at night to every detail in between, like how to answer the phone, how to make appointments, and how to track the money. It also includes details such as the appearance of the lobby, the cleanliness of the kitchen, the Internet connection in the conference rooms, the client appreciation events, the duties of the nightly cleaning crew, the media relations, and so forth. This specificity organizes your firm to such a degree that it frees you from being caught inside it.

Succeeding at the next level means stepping out of your business and delegating tasks to others. I've met many highly qualified, intelligent financial advisors who could never envision trusting others to get the job done. A messiah complex is a roadblock. Don't get me wrong. You can fly in from time to time and sit with clients or intervene where necessary. But there's no reason why you should be stuck at the copy machine when you don't have to be.

To get to your destination faster, you have to clear out and clearly define your path. Ron Rothgeb once said, "I asked for a life raft and they threw me a yacht!" I love this quote because it illustrates the universe's positive forces at work on our behalf when we simply seek them.

Thanks to planning, you can become a leader in your marketplace. Here are **Twelve Steps to Dominating Your Marketplace** that can take you to the top:

1. Business Vision. Outline exactly what you do for your clients and make sure everything is in harmony with your value system. Don't do something just to make a sale or collect a commission or fee. Believe in everything you do. When you do the right thing, the money will come.

2. The Five Pillars of Strength in Marketing. Identify your market by asking five key questions: who, what, when, where, and why. Then establish the five pillars of strength of your choice to support your marketing plan. For example, common pillars might include seminars, direct mail, Internet/web, and professional relationships with both CPAs and attorneys. Choose the pillars that fit your marketing plan best.

Also put effort into becoming branded. Advertise on a regular basis and make sure all of your marketing is cohesive. For instance, make sure that every marketing piece has your company logo, a slogan, and possibly your picture. When I do newspaper or magazine ads, I generally opt for full-page ads. I scouted one local publication in my area that everybody reads and purchased the back cover space or the inside front cover every month for two to three years. Eventually, people came up to me to say, "You're the guy I see in that magazine all the time." That's how you brand yourself.

Postcards can also be effective. Even in the Internet era, turning out 10,000 to 30,000 postcards a month with a picture on each one generates a good response.

3. The Appointment Process. In my company, we write out everything we say to a client, from the opening or warm-up to the fact finder, which is the data form we collect. We script the topics we discuss and the illustrations that might be handy for prospective clients. We even write out in about six to eight pages what to say as we walk clients through our proprietary software, which calculates the clients' money and maps out how they can retire safely. We also write down what to say as we do survivorship planning, discuss life insurance, and make sure the beneficiaries are lined up correctly.

Many advisors wing the first appointment, but that's not professional. If you refer to the same script every time and it works, then you should keep using it.

4. Client Fulfillment. Moving money for a client involves a hefty process. Client fulfillment means making sure that each step in the delivery process is strategically passed through staff to ensure every detail is accurate and verified. When a client has an account with "ABC" company and we're moving it from "ABC" company to us, there are many forms that need to be signed plus an entire process to go along with each form. Then sometimes, you'll get a client who shows up with sixteen or eighteen different accounts, and you spend time consolidating them into six or eight accounts.

Every step in the delivery process should be written out in the procedure manuals. I have four or five people who each oversee a specific function within the delivery process. Every year, I move between $30 million to $60 million into our firm. Then applications for life insurance and other processes that require underwriting take even more time. Every step is important, and you have to know and outline what happens at every turn so that you don't drop the ball at the goal line before you score.

5. Client for Life Communication. I believe that when you obtain a client, you obtain him or her for life. Aim to keep the relationship for as long as the client lives. Create a system to remain connected with each client and his or her beneficiaries through annual reviews, newsletters, invitations to client seminars, contacts on anniversary dates, client appreciation events, and guest speaker events with people like Ed Slott or Michael E. Gerber. If you do a good job, you may have even made money for your children who will inherit the client after you.

6. Residual Income/Found Money. There are those who go after only residual income and those who go after only first-year commissions. We go after a mixture of both. It's important to keep track of the renewals you receive or the annual fees that you charge. Also keep tabs on the money you will acquire when clients retire, inherit money, or pass away. There's always money in motion and you have to stay connected and babysit the money that is waiting for a client's retirement or someone's death until it's ready to come out. Many advisors drop the ball because they don't stay in touch with their clients often enough. I do semiannual reviews (twice a year) so clients get a chance to come in and we can revive the relationship on a regular basis.

7. Strategic Partnerships. Surprisingly, this is the area that stumps most businesspeople. Strategic partnerships are formed with professionals in the community with whom you choose to do business on an ongoing basis. These are the people who will help you build your practice through referrals and strategic marketing. The reason this is tougher than it seems is because when you're dealing with high-end professionals, they will ask you tough questions and challenge your business. They will ask questions that make you stretch, learn, and grow. But if you are open to these challenges and relationships, these are the people who will give you some of your most valuable personal introductions.

8. Information Technology. Make sure your IT works properly, is protected, and is up to date with the latest tools, programs, and documents. The better you adapt to technology, the easier it will be to run your business. Embracing new technology is what will help you stay ahead of your competition. This also communicates to your clients and business associates that you continually invest in your firm.

You'd be surprised how many business professionals don't have a Web site for their company. There are relatively cheap programs that can help you construct a simple Web site. If you are affiliated with a broker dealer, ask him or her to help you market through every possible compliance-approved contact and social networking sites such as Facebook, LinkedIn, Twitter, and YouTube. Today, the people who don't invest in technology are the ones who will be replaced.

9. Accounting and Forecasting. Dive into the books to analyze cash flow and profitability. You have to know what's coming in and what's going out of your business. Working in a commissions or fee-based environment is trickier because you can't control when you get paid.

In the industry, the average number of days it takes to get paid on an annuity sale is forty-five days, but in our company we sped up our process to make that number twenty-eight days. I went through and asked my employees to explain how things work. I asked, "What does he do? Then what happens? Does it sit on his desk? Is it sent out that day or the next day? When it's sent out the next day, does the person open it that day or the day after that?" Then I suggested that we tighten the time frame between sending and opening, which we did in about seven different ways until we were able to shave off two to three weeks of our process. This attention to detail can make the difference between having the money to do your next marketing campaign and not having the money to market.

10. Staff Management and Accountability. Managing staff requires making sure you match up skill sets with the proper employees who possess those skill sets. We'll discuss monitoring and managing your staff further in the next chapter.

11. Continuing Education. Continuing education includes special coaching, mentoring, study groups, and industry functions. A frightening majority of adults believe they already know every-thing they'll ever need to know. But getting ahead and staying ahead requires constant learning. Obtain at least the minimum license and training required for your practice. When you work with a trainer, don't go for the minimum; press ahead to the next level.

I've always pressed ahead to the next level. But what I've found is that most organizations only pay for the minimum and say that the rest is on your dime. Don't let this deter you. I'd rather invest in myself than in something else. Over the years, I've paid hundreds of thousands of dollars to receive the best training from the best people in the business. In fact, more than once, somebody has said to me, "I read this guy's book," and I'll say, "Well, I have his phone number. Let's give him a call." I know I paid that guy $15,000 to hear him speak and I feel comfortable calling him up. This concept baffles a lot of people, but it has made me a million dollars.

12. Ancillary Business System. Seek out multiple revenue streams through affiliations with people in your industry to add to your bottom line and build your brand. For example, I once said to my staff, "We're sitting on $5 million to $10 million in life insurance premiums." They disagreed, so I brought in an associate who places high-end life insurance. I told the staff that when we brought him in, we'd close six figures in premiums in one day. Sure enough, we closed six figures in one day in premiums.

Bringing in an expert can generate lots of revenue. If I line up the right people with my specialty, which is income planning and annuities/life insurance, I know I can place $2 million of annuities/ life insurance every day in any state in the country. This would make the company I help a lot of money and it would generally split the profit with me fifty-fifty, as I did with my friend who came in.

Multiple revenue streams are everywhere. Even when your practice is multidisciplinary, you still have a specialty; something you're the best at. Think of it as the lowest-hanging fruit. If you focus on managed money and you're not looking into life insurance or annuities, you should call someone who specializes in those other disciplines to take in an extra $200,000 to $1 million a year. I once heard somebody say, "God's trying to hand you diamonds, but you won't let go of the rubies." Sometimes, it's important to devote your attention to your specialty and bring in people who can help you generate more income in the other areas.

These twelve steps plus the three types of planning provide you with the blueprint you need to transform your business from its current state to the next level. This blueprint minimizes those endless to-do lists while making sure every step is well thought out and monitored to stay updated and compliant.

You are now free to put all these ideas into action and embark on the most exciting journey of your life. You're no longer limited within your business. You're taking the reins to control your business from outside. Now that your plan is coming together, we need to hear what Michael E. Gerber has to say about management. ✤

CHAPTER 7

On the Subject
of Management

Michael E. Gerber

Good management consists of showing average people how to do the
work of superior people.

—John D. Rockefeller

Every financial advisor, including Steve, eventually faces the issue of management. Most face it badly.

Why do so many financial advisors suffer from a kind of paralysis when it comes to dealing with management? Why are so few able to get their financial advisory practice to work the way they want it to and to run it on time? Why are their managers (if they have any) seemingly so inept?

There are two main problems. First, the financial advisor usually abdicates accountability for management by hiring an office manager. Thus, the financial advisor is working hand and glove with someone who is supposed to do the managing. But the financial advisor is unmanageable himself!

The financial advisor doesn't think like a manager because he doesn't think he is a manager. He's a financial advisor! He rules the roost. And so he gets the office manager to take care of stuff like scheduling appointments, keeping his calendar, collecting receivables, hiring/firing, and much more.

Second, no matter who does the managing, they usually have a completely dysfunctional idea of what it means to manage. They're trying to manage people, contrary to what is needed.

We often hear that a good manager must be a "people person." Someone who loves to nourish, figure out, support, care for, teach, baby, monitor, mentor, direct, track, motivate, and, if all else fails, threaten or beat up her people.

Don't believe it. Management has far less to do with people than you've been led to believe.

In fact, despite the claims of every management book written by management gurus (who have seldom managed anything), no one— with the exception of a few bloodthirsty tyrants—has ever learned how to manage people.

And the reason is simple: *People are almost impossible to manage.*

Yes, it's true. People are unmanageable. They're inconsistent, unpredictable, unchangeable, unrepentant, irrepressible, and generally impossible.

Doesn't knowing this make you feel better? Now you understand why you've had all those problems! Do you feel the relief, the heavy stone lifted from your chest?

The time has come to fully understand what management is really all about. Rather than managing *people*, management is really all about managing a *process*, a step-by-step way of doing things, which, combined with other processes, becomes a system. For example:

- The process for on-time scheduling
- The process for answering the telephone
- The process for greeting a client
- The process for organizing client files

Thus, a process is the step-by-step way of doing something over time. Considered as a whole, these processes are a system:

- The on-time scheduling system
- The telephone answering system
- The client greeting system
- The file organization system

Instead of managing people, then, the truly effective manager has been taught a system for managing a process through which people get things done.

More precisely, managers and their people, *together*, manage the processes—the systems—that comprise your business. Management is less about *who* gets things done in your business than about *how* things get done.

In fact, great managers are not fascinated with people, but with how things get done through people. Great managers are masters at figuring out how to get things done effectively and efficiently through people using extraordinary systems.

Great managers constantly ask key questions, such as:

- What is the result we intend to produce?
- Are we producing that result every single time?
- If we're not producing that result every single time, why not?
- If we are producing that result every single time, how could we produce even better results?
- Do we lack a system? If so, what would that system look like if we were to create it?
- If we have a system, why aren't we using it?

And so forth.

In short, a great manager can leave the office fully assured that it will run at least as well as it does when he or she is physically in the room.

Great managers are those who use a great management system. A system that shouts, "This is *how* we manage here." Not, "This is *who* manages here."

In a truly effective company, how you manage is always more important than who manages. Provided a system is in place, how you manage is transferable, whereas who manages isn't. *How* you manage can be taught, whereas *who* manages can't be.

When a company is dependent on *who* manages—Janet, Jill, or Joe—that business is in serious jeopardy. Because when Janet, Jill, or Joe leaves, that business has to start over again. What an enormous waste of time and resources!

Even worse, when a company is dependent on *who* manages, you can bet all the managers in that business are doing their own thing. What could be more unproductive than ten managers who each manage in a unique way? How in the world could you possibly manage those managers?

The answer is: You can't. Because it takes you right back to trying to manage *people* again.

And, as I hope you now know, that's impossible.

In this chapter, I often refer to managers in the plural. I know that most financial advisors only have one manager—the office manager. And so you may be thinking that a management system isn't so important in a small financial advisory practice. After all, the office manager does whatever an office manager does (and thank God, because you don't want to do it).

But if your practice is ever going to turn into the business it could become, and if that business is ever going to turn into the enterprise of your dreams, then the questions you ask about how the office manager manages your affairs are critical ones. Because until you come to grips with your dual role as owner and key employee, and the relationship your manager has to those two roles, your practice/business/enterprise will never realize its potential. Thus the need for a management system.

Management System

What, then, is a management system?

The E-Myth says that a management system is the method by which every manager innovates, quantifies, orchestrates, and then monitors the systems through which your practice produces the results you expect.

According to the E-Myth, a manager's job is simple:

A manager's job is to invent the systems through which the owner's vision is consistently and faithfully manifested at the operating level of the business.

Which brings us right back to the purpose of your business and the need for an entrepreneurial vision.

Are you beginning to see what I'm trying to share with you? That your business is one single thing? And that all the subjects we're discussing here—money, planning, management, and so on—are all about doing one thing well?

That one thing is the one thing your practice is intended to do: distinguish your financial advisory business from all others.

It is the manager's role to make certain it all fits. And it's your role as entrepreneur to make sure your manager knows what the business is supposed to look, act, and feel like when it's finally done. As clearly as you know how, you must convey to your manager what you know to be true—your vision, your picture of the business when it's finally done. In this way, your vision is translated into your manager's marching orders every day he or she reports to work.

Unless that vision is embraced by your manager, you and your people will suffer from the tyranny of routine. And your business will suffer from it, too.

Now let's move on to *people*. Because, as we know, it's people who are causing all our problems. But before we do, let's hear what Michael Steranka has to say about management. ✤

CHAPTER

8

Managing the Unmanageable

Michael Steranka

Motivation is what gets you started. Habit is what keeps you going.
—Jim Rohn

One sentence from Michael E. Gerber permanently changed the way I approach management: *People are not manageable, but systems are.*

I can't explain the relief that overcame me when I figured this out. My epiphany was profound. I had read at least a hundred books on management, attended countless workshops, and paid a number of consultants to coach me on management. But nothing worked because I was trying to manage the unmanageable.

Employees are human. Humans have good days and bad days. We have days when we whistle on the way to the office and nights when we want to punch the wall. We experience every emotion in the spectrum and are influenced by our children, our parents, and the guy who cut us off in traffic. Sometimes we show up to work sick. Sometimes we're forced to stay home. We live through births, deaths, and divorces. We have spouses who love us. We have spouses who leave us. Various addictions can haunt families, like alcoholism or drugs. Our children and parents need our attention, and so do our spouses.

And we think we can manage all of those events and run a business? It's a wonder we get any employees to show up at all.

I can't effectively control somebody's moods, behaviors, or actions. But I can measure and manage the system. For example, I can determine whether the lights were turned on, the copies were made, the applications were processed, or the mail was sent. And if I can measure those duties, then I know that the employee who turned on the lights, made the copies, processed the applications, and sent the mail did his job. Likewise, I can determine who did not do his job by measuring which of those jobs weren't accomplished.

Measuring and monitoring systems works because systems are more black and white than people, whose behaviors shift every day. If I come into the office and I find an employee sitting in the dark, I know immediately that he did not turn on the lights. As you E-Myth your business, most items will become as obvious to you as the lights being off. Then you'll see just as plain as day who is being productive within your company and who isn't.

At our company, we've established a procedures manual to determine what we want to hold our staff accountable for. This manual includes the details for every function and every occupation in the company. For example, the operations manager has a clear outline of everything that falls under operations. I have a processor, file prep person, money mover person, receptionist, marketing person, and two assistants. Each person oversees specific functions. I don't expect my employees to tell me what they're best at and what they'd like to accomplish. I have a manual that clearly lays out what each role entails.

When I hire someone, I try to match up the skill sets this person has with those defined in the procedures manual. This process makes it easy to figure out when we don't have the right person in a particular position. The mismatch shows up relatively quickly, sometimes within a week. When a new hire doesn't work out, the others in the company will pick up on it right away, and will say that this person doesn't have a clue and is gumming up the works.

A company is similar to an assembly line. If I pass an assignment to Bob and Bob passes it to Sue but Bob drops the ball, then Sue will call me to say, "Bob didn't do this right so I can't do my job right." Then we can approach Bob, take a look at Bob's procedures manual to figure out what went wrong, and make a change if necessary.

This measurable approach allows you to keep your staff accountable without letting personalities get in the way. When people know what's expected of them, they're freed to do their jobs while also being able to be whatever version of their personalities they need to be that day. This prevents likeable people who are somewhat amiable but incompetent from hanging around, and also prevents people who may not be that vibrant from getting fired. When you manage systems instead of people, you begin to hire and fire and manage based on productivity and progress, instead of on emotion or other human factors.

Now let's take a step back. If you are in the stage in which you're doing all the managing and systematizing with no employees to hold accountable, begin by holding *yourself* accountable.

Take an honest look at where you are in terms of production. What was your cash flow over the last two years? Create a realistic chart for yourself and ask, "Am I taking too much time off?" "Do I have a solid marketing plan?" "Do I make enough calls?" "Do my clients even know that I'm alive and still in business?" Measure where you are now in your business, where you've been, and what your current expenses are. That's snapshot number one.

Snapshot number two is a new action plan. Refer to the last chapter about planning and use it to create a 90-day action plan that will help you turn your ship around. You can't turn it around overnight, but if you strategically plan what practices you'll use and what steps you'll take to change the direction of your business, you can right the ship in a matter of ninety days or a year, or in whatever time span you set for yourself.

If you have a smaller shop and have nobody working for you, your first hire should be an assistant. I recommend finding someone who possesses a license but can't sell. This person will know how to do the paperwork and thanks to the license, he or she will be able to talk to clients when you're not around and at least keep the conversation going until you return.

Your second hire should be a marketing person who doubles as a receptionist. These are two different functions, but if you're working on a shoestring, you'll initially have everybody perform multiple functions. There was a time when I oversaw and performed every function in my procedures manual. Then the duties were split between me and someone else, and then four people shared the work. Now I need about eight or ten people to accomplish everything really efficiently.

Eventually, you'll scale out the duties and positions depending on how much growth you want. You might need two people to do this and three people to do that. But eventually, you'll get to a level at which you've got somebody different handling every function.

Have you ever gotten frustrated at the office? Have you ever made a fool of yourself in front of your staff or even your clients? Have you ever thought you were going crazy? If you're a human being with your own set of personal issues and you're trying to manage a team of other very human employees, meltdowns not only occur, but are expected. But when you begin to manage systems and you learn to monitor these systems effectively, your meltdowns should all but disappear.

Because you are deeply invested in your company, the temptation will be to try to manage personalities and people as you mentor and work with the associates in the office. Don't worry about whether the people are right. Just make sure the system is right. Then you'll be able to weed out the people who should be fired from the people you need to keep. Management is less about employing the right people and more about employing the right people who will get the right jobs done.

Congratulations. You covered a lot of ground in the previous chapters. Let's take a look as Michael E. Gerber teaches us about people in the next chapter. ✤

CHAPTER

9

On the Subject
of People

Michael E. Gerber

Very few people go to the doctor when they have a cold. They go to the
theatre instead.

—Oscar Wilde

E very financial advisor I've ever met has complained about people.
About employees: "They come in late, they go home
early, they have the focus of an antique camera!"

About insurance companies: "They're living in a nonparallel universe!"

About clients: "They want me to repair years of bad spending habits and decades of investment indifference and then they want me to tell them they can take a lot of risk and still never run out of money."

People, people, people. Every financial advisor's nemesis. And at the heart of it all are the people who work for you.

"By the time I tell them how to do it, I could have done it twenty times myself!" "How come nobody listens to what I say?" "Why is it nobody ever does what I ask them to do?" Does this sound like you?

So what's the problem with people? To answer that, think back to the last time you walked into a financial advisor's office. What did you see in the people's faces?

Most people working in financial advisory are harried. You can see it in their expressions. They're negative. They're bad-spirited. They're humorless. And with good reason. After all, they're surrounded by people who have done a poor job handling their own money and are nervous and suspicious because they have had negative experiences for the most part with other advisors. Clients are looking for nurturing, for empathy, for care. And many are either terrified or depressed. They don't want to be there.

Is it any wonder employees at most financial advisory practices are disgruntled? They're surrounded by nervous people all day. They're answering the same questions 24/7. And most of the time, the financial advisor has no time for them. He or she is too busy leading a dysfunctional life.

Working with people brings great joy—and monumental frustration. And so it is with financial advisors and their people. But why? And what can we do about it?

Let's look at the typical financial advisor—who this person is and isn't.

Most financial advisors are unprepared to use other people to get results. Not because they can't find people, but because they are fixated on getting the results themselves. In other words, most financial advisors are not the businesspeople they need to be, but *technicians suffering from an entrepreneurial seizure.*

Am I talking about you? What were you doing before you became an entrepreneur?

Were you an associate financial advisor working for a large multi-office organization? A midsized practice? A small practice?

Didn't you imagine owning your own practice as the way out?

Didn't you think that because you knew how to do the technical work—because you knew so much about financial planning—that you were automatically prepared to create a practice that does that type of work?

Didn't you figure that by creating your own practice, you could dump the boss once and for all? How else to get rid of that impossible person, the one driving you crazy, the one who never let you do your own thing, the one who was the main reason you decided to take the leap into a business of your own in the first place?

Didn't you start your own practice so that you could become your own boss?

And didn't you imagine that once you became your own boss, you would be free to do whatever you wanted to do—and to take home *all* the money?

Honestly, isn't that what you imagined? So you went into business for yourself and immediately dived into work.

Doing it, doing it, doing it.

Busy, busy, busy.

Until one day you realized (or maybe not) that you were doing all of the work. You were doing everything you knew how to do, plus a lot more you knew nothing about. Building sweat equity, you thought.

In reality, a technician suffering from an entrepreneurial seizure.

You were just hoping to make a buck in your own practice. And sometimes you did earn a wage. But other times you didn't. You were the one signing the checks, all right, but they went to other people.

Does this sound familiar? Is it driving you crazy?

Well, relax, because we're going to show you the right way to do it this time.

Read carefully. Be mindful of the moment. You are about to learn the secret you've been waiting for all your working life.

The People Law

It's critical to know this about the working life of financial advisors who own their own financial advisory practice: *Without people, you don't own a practice, you own a job.* And it can be the worst job in the world because you're working for a lunatic! (Nothing personal—but we've got to face facts.)

Let me state what every financial advisor knows: Without people, you're going to have to do it all yourself. Without human help, you're doomed to try to do too much. This isn't a breakthrough idea, but it's amazing how many financial advisors ignore the truth. They end up knocking themselves out, ten to twelve hours a day. They try to do more, but less actually gets done.

The load can double you over and leave you panting. In addition to the work you're used to doing, you may also have to do the books. And the organizing. And the filing. You'll have to do the planning and the scheduling. When you own your own practice, the daily minutiae are never-ceasing—as I'm sure you've found out. Like painting the Golden Gate Bridge, it's endless. Which puts it beyond the realm of human possibility. Until you discover how to get it done by somebody else, it will continue on and on until you're a burned-out husk.

But with others helping you, things will start to drastically improve. If, that is, you truly understand how to engage people in the work you need them to do. When you learn how to do that, when you learn how to replace yourself with other people—people trained in your system—then your practice can really begin to grow. Only then will you begin to experience true freedom yourself.

What typically happens is that financial advisors, knowing they need help answering the phone, filing, and so on, go out and find people who can do these things. Once they delegate these duties, however, they rarely spend any time with the employee. Deep down they feel it's not important *how* these things get done; it's only important that they get done.

They fail to grasp the requirement for a system that makes people their greatest asset rather than their greatest liability. A system so reliable that if Chris dropped dead tomorrow, Leslie could do exactly what Chris did. That's where the People Law comes in.

*The People Law says that each time you add a new person
to your practice using an intelligent (turnkey) system that works,*

you expand your reach. And you can expand your reach almost infinitely! People allow you to be everywhere you want to be simultaneously, without actually having to be there in the flesh.

People are to a financial advisor what a record was to Frank Sinatra. A Sinatra record could be (and still is) played in a million places at the same time, regardless of where Frank was. And every record sale produced royalties for Sinatra (or his estate).

With the help of other people, Sinatra created a quality recording that faithfully replicated his unique talents, then made sure it was marketed, distributed, and the revenue managed.

Your people can do the same thing for you. All *you* need to do is to create a "recording"—a system—of your unique talents, your special way of practicing financial advisory, and then replicate it, market it, distribute it, and manage the revenue.

Isn't that what successful businesspeople do? Make a "recording" of their most effective ways of doing business? In this way, they provide a turnkey solution to their clients' problems. A system solution that really works.

Doesn't your practice offer the same potential for you that records did for Frank Sinatra (and now for his heirs)? The ability to produce income without having to go to work every day?

Isn't that what your people could be for you? The means by which your system for practicing financial advisory could be faithfully replicated?

But first you've got to have a system. You have to create a unique way of doing business that you can teach to your people, that you can manage faithfully, and that you can replicate consistently, just like McDonald's.

Because without such a system, without such a "recording," without a unique way of doing business that really works, all you're left with is people doing their own thing. And that is almost always a recipe for chaos. Rather than guaranteeing consistency, it encourages mistake after mistake after mistake.

And isn't that how the problem started in the first place? People doing whatever *they* perceived they needed to do, regardless of what you wanted? People left to their own devices, with no regard for the costs of their behavior? The costs to you?

In other words, people without a system.

Can you imagine what would have happened to Frank Sinatra if he had followed that example? If every one of his recordings had been done differently? Imagine a million different versions of "My Way." It's unthinkable.

Would you buy a record like that? What if Frank was having a bad day? What if he had a sore throat?

Please hear this: The People Law is unforgiving. Without a systematic way of doing business, people are more often a liability than an asset. Unless you prepare, you'll find out too late which ones are which.

The People Law says that without a specific system for doing business; without a specific system for recruiting, hiring, and training your people to use that system; and without a specific system for managing and improving your systems, your practice will always be a crapshoot.

Do you want to roll the dice with your practice at stake? Unfortunately, that is what most financial advisors are doing.

The People Law also says that you can't effectively delegate your responsibilities unless you have something specific to delegate. And that something specific is a way of doing business that works!

Frank Sinatra is gone, but his voice lives on. And someone is still counting his royalties. That's because Sinatra had a system that worked.

Do you? Now let's move on to the subject of associate financial advisors. But first, let's listen to what Michael Steranka has to say about people. ✤

CHAPTER 10

People Needing People

Michael Steranka

Playoffs? Playoffs? You're talking about playoffs?
—Jim Mora, former coach, New Orleans Saints

Have you ever worked with a five o'clocker? You know the type. You finish with a client late because you have to, and you need assistance so you buzz the desk of one of your people. But it's 5:15 p.m. and he's gone. You've just buzzed the desk of a five o'clocker. In fact, you would have missed him even if you had buzzed him at 5:02 p.m.

Five o'clockers usually stop working around 4:00 p.m. in the afternoon. They avoid starting important tasks past 4:40 p.m. because they have plans that don't include you, your firm, or your clients. This late in the day, the worst of them will even hang up on a call if they are on hold and then report to you that the person you wanted to reach is already gone for the day.

These days, most five o'clockers are unemployed, but sometimes, a few of them do such a fantastic job pretending to be invested employees that you don't identify them until after they've been hired and have been with you for some time.

So is it that much of a problem to have a five o'clocker or two on your staff? And if you don't want five o'clockers working for you, then whom should you hire? This chapter will answer these questions and discuss the importance of the people who will become the final spoke you need in your wheel once you have your systems in place.

Talking about the people you need for your business is tricky because there is no set formula for how many people you need except as your business plan would dictate. A general rule of thumb is to have one support person for every one hundred to two hundred accounts or households. So if you have eight hundred accounts, employing at least four support personnel would be a good idea. The reason for this is simple: Good customer service means good client retention, and we know it's much easier to retain a client than it is to acquire a new one.

Client retention is crucial because a good client can and will refer at least one new client to you every two years. Keep a client for ten years and he or she can introduce you to five others, who will in turn generate at least five more clients over that same time span.

Client retention requires adding value to the relationship you have with that client through advice, knowledge, service, and product. Having the right support personnel to aid this process is essential. Listen to your staff when they are on the phone with clients or prospective clients. Observe how well they handle each situation and address any necessary changes immediately.

I've had a wide variety of people work for me, from great people to good people, average people to poor people. I find that people with average or poor skill sets never make it past the one-year mark. Sometimes, the good also become average or poor, so it is important to issue strong suggestions or warnings when necessary.

Never hesitate to replace a weak link. A person with a poor attitude or inadequate skill set is like a cancer. He or she must be cut out immediately. That bad attitude can be contagious, not only to the other people in the office, but also to your clients. I would rather leave the phone ringing than have a negative employee give a false impression of our firm to a prospective or current client.

Hiring clients can also be an option. Clients also can be a source of great referrals. They already understand you and you know whether you like them. Just make sure they bring valuable skill sets to the table and consider how they would fit in. Maybe this client would be the perfect receptionist. Or maybe your client could help at a seminar. Maybe one has an accounting background and could work as a tax preparer. I've employed clients who have ended up working for me for years.

Now that we've discussed why it's important to hire the right people, let's discuss exactly what kind of people you need.

I break up my staff into four categories: *reception, marketing, sales,* and *support.*

Reception. One person can generally handle the reception duties, but these duties are key to your business. This means that this one person can make or break you. In my firm, we have one person at the front desk, but we also have three people who are trained and ready to staff the front desk on an as-needed basis.

Employing an excellent person in the reception area is crucial to our firm because we hold all of our appointments in our office. We don't make house calls because if people don't value what we do enough to come see us at our place of business, then they're communicating that they don't value our time.

The person at your reception desk makes the first physical contact with a prospective client. He or she is also the first voice on the phone that represents your firm to the public. And as the old adage goes, you have just one chance at a first impression.

We deal primarily with millionaires and multimillionaires, and I've been in the business long enough to know that I've landed and lost deals because of first impressions. Don't forget that first impressions work both ways. You can make the mistake of prejudging an individual and then completely altering your impression of that person after you uncover some important facts about him or her. I've been pleasantly surprised by new introductions to the firm many times.

People who work in the reception area are almost akin to salespeople in that they need many of the same skill sets, plus an additional one that many sales people don't have: organization. Your systems must be equipped with a client management database that is large enough to handle the job, yet accessible enough for the less tech-savvy people in the firm to manage. More than five thousand people have attended my seminars, and we are constantly updating and purging our list.

I've had average receptionists who cost me small fortunes by way of missed opportunities, wrong scheduling, overbooking, and the like. The bottom line is this: Select well, monitor often, and reward when warranted.

Marketing. Our marketing department has one to three people in it at any given time. We outsource the marketing as much as possible, but we've learned to keep certain things in house because of the proprietary nature of our marketing efforts. Some marketing people can't be trusted, some are incompetent, and some simply don't care.

My current marketing person is one of my favorite people. I love the excellent ways she always looks to improve the business, cut costs, and reach out for new marketing alliances.

Marketing people must be able to be nice when needed, as well as firm or even abrupt on occasion. Many people will attempt to waste your marketing person's time, but don't let them. Protect your marketing person's time as though it is your own.

Make sure to employ marketing people who have a thick skin. Not every marketing tactic works smoothly, and the people in charge generally receive little glory and all of the blame. Marketing is a constantly evolving game. What worked ten years ago may work differently today, so it is your marketing person's job to stay on top of things and see where trends go in the marketplace.

Building a brand is not as difficult as you might expect, but if you don't know where to spend your marketing dollars, you will go broke before anyone knows your name. Make sure your marketing person knows when to take risks or go against the grain.

Your marketing person is the brain behind the brand. Every day, someone who you may not know is referred to you. And it's the marketing person who helps those prospective clients know you before they meet you, or at least think they know you.

Sales. Somewhat of a misnomer, "sales" refers more to addressing the needs and concerns of the client. I love sales. I love selling people on the merits of doing business with us and I love selling the plans that will solve the issues people worry about. Over the years, I made it a point to be in front of as many people with money as possible. I took notes. I asked people why they didn't become clients. I learned to talk less and listen more. I learned to talk a lot less, and really, *really* listen.

People will tell you what they want. I want to repeat that: People will tell you what they want. As a salesperson, you simply need to show them how what you have matches up with what they want. If they like you and what you have matches up with what they want, then you will gain a new client.

Never take it personally when someone decides not to become a client. This is strictly a business decision. Once you view the interaction that way, you can confidently shake hands at the beginning and at the end of the meeting even if there is no chance that this person will do business with you. This mentality also helps you move quickly to the next prospective client.

Many people are blindly naïve about their finances. Others who think they have their finances figured out actually don't know much. But it is difficult to confront another person about his or her money and tell him as politely as possible that he or she doesn't have a clue. I have no problem doing this because I believe in what I do—right down to my core. When you believe in what you do, selling becomes much easier.

The other day, I was talking to a gentleman worth $100 million in investments and he told me that his number one concern is running out of money. I have come to learn that whether they have $1 million or a $100 million, most people have one identical concern: running out of money. The quality of life among these people may differ, but their feelings are the same.

Many clients have told me that I am like their therapist. I've definitely maneuvered through minefields with some clients. Maybe one client is bad with money or maybe it's her husband. Maybe she takes too much risk and he's too conservative. I find that most times, if you can get couples to agree on a few fundamental truths about their money, then they will start to see the logic of working together in harmony as opposed to working against each other, or worse, working in secret from each other.

Learning about sales should be an ongoing concern. You can never learn enough, never retain enough, never close every single deal. But you sure can give it your best effort. I enjoy learning about sales and about what my peers are doing or not doing. If someone does more business than I do, I think of it as an opportunity to learn. I have many people doing less than me who have taught me invaluable lessons, as well. So always remain teachable.

Some people have an innate ability when it comes to sales. I remember meeting one top sales professional who said I was a natural. I took the remark as a compliment, but what he didn't see was that I wasn't an overnight sensation. I was twenty years in the making.

Books are written every day about sales and the psychology of sales. For the most part, you can throw those books out. Selling is the art of guiding a potential prospect from where he is now to where he needs to be. If that place is better than where he is now, you have a client. If not, don't worry about it.

Support. The support staff is the area in which most advisors make the mistake of trying to save a few dollars. Your support staff is the glue that holds the firm together. This is the place to spend the money. Our support staff is four to six people strong, and each person brings valuable assets to the table. Some of the tasks our support staff oversee daily are the following:

- Compiling asset summary reports with current market values
- Creating Morningstar reports on fund positions inside 401(k) plans
- Generating net worth statements

- Making life insurance illustrations
- Making annuity illustrations
- Making long-term care illustrations
- Filling out asset transfer forms
- Filling out ACAT transfer forms
- Making calls to custodians to verify transfers
- Tracking transfers
- Making trades
- Tracking RMDs on all clients seventy-and-a-half years old
- Putting financial plans together in binders
- Delivering binders
- Getting all PDRs on life and annuity deliveries
- Receiving checks from clients
- Delivering checks to clients
- Retitling assets in the name of the trust
- Checking beneficiary forms annually
- Answering questions for clients and beneficiaries of accounts
- Meeting with clients and family members
- Greeting clients and beneficiaries
- Making copies and scanning in copies of new accounts
- Organizing and setting up new files
- Keeping fresh coffee and refreshments for clients all day
- Keeping the kitchen area clean
- Helping clients with non-asset-related issues
- Referring attorneys or CPAs, when needed
- Dealing with banks and mortgage companies for verification
- Explaining renewal features on indexed annuities
- Updating passwords for clients on E-Money

Your support staff has countless opportunities a day to make you look like a hero or a goat. With the proper systems to measure these

86 *The E-Myth Financial Advisor*

functions, you can easily monitor results. Without those systems, you will spend the majority of your time chasing your tail.

People are essential, and it's important to find good-quality, stable people who are not job-hoppers. Of course, I ideally want these good people to stay with me forever. But on occasion, when one needs to fly the coop, you have no choice but to let him or her go. Good people always leave on good terms. If they leave on less-than-good terms, maybe they were actually average or poor people pretending to be good or great.

The systems you put in place will ferret out the great from the not-so-great. Their performance will be exemplary and they will often ask what else they can do. Hold on to these people. They are diamonds who are worth a fortune to your firm. Cherish them, reward them, and include them in the profits. You never know whether these people are the ones who will buy the firm they've helped you build when you are ready to sell.

Now let's see what Michael E. Gerber has to say about associates. ✤

CHAPTER

11

On the Subject of Associates

Michael E. Gerber

Associate yourself with men of good quality if you esteem your own reputation, for 'tis better to be alone than in bad company.

—George Washington

If you're a sole practitioner—that is, you're selling only yourself— then your financial advisory company called a practice will never make the leap to a financial advisory company called a business. The progression from practice to business to enterprise demands that you hire other financial advisors to do what you do (or don't do). Contractors call these people subcontractors; for our purposes, we'll refer to them as associate financial advisors.

Contractors know that subs can be a huge problem. It's no less true for financial advisors. Until you face this special business problem, your practice will never become a business, and your business will certainly never become an enterprise.

Long ago, God said, "Let there be financial advisors. And so they never forget who they are in my creation, let them

87

be damned forever to hire people exactly like themselves." Enter the associates.

Merriam-Webster's Collegiate Dictionary, Eleventh Edition, defines *sub* as "under, below, secretly; inferior to." If associate financial advisors are like sub-financial advisors, you could define an associate as "an inferior individual contracted to perform part or all of another's contract."

In other words, you, the financial advisor, make a conscious decision to hire someone "inferior" to you to fulfill *your* commitment to *your* client, for which you are ultimately and solely liable.

Why in the world do we do these things to ourselves? Where will this madness lead? It seems the blind are leading the blind, and the blind are paying others to do it. And when a financial advisor is blind, you *know* there's a problem!

It's time to step out of the darkness and come into the light. Forget about being Mr. Nice Guy—it's time to do things that work.

Solving the Associate Financial Advisor Problem

Let's say you're about to hire an associate financial advisor. Someone who has specific skills: closing new clients, making excellent presentation skills, or explaining complex terms to clients in creative ways. It all starts with choosing the right personnel. After all, these are people to whom you are delegating your responsibility and for whose behavior you are completely liable. Do you really want to leave that choice to chance? Are you that much of a gambler? I doubt it.

If you've never worked with your new associate, how do you really know he or she is skilled? For that matter, what does "skilled" mean?

For you to make an intelligent decision about this associate financial advisor, you must have a working definition of the word *skilled*. Your challenge is to know *exactly* what your expectations are, then to make sure your other financial advisors operate with precisely the same expectations. Failure here almost assures a break-down in your relationship.

I want you to write the following on a piece of paper: "By *skilled*, I mean . . ." Once you create your personal definition, it will become a standard for you and your practice, for your clients, and for your associate financial advisors.

A standard, according to *Webster's Eleventh*, is something "set up and established by authority as a rule for the measure of quantity, weight, extent, value, or quality."

Thus, your goal is to establish a measure of quality control, a standard of skill, which you will apply to all your associate financial advisors. More important, you are also setting a standard for the performance of your company.

By creating standards for your selection of other financial advi-sors—standards of skill, performance, integrity, financial stability, and experience—you have begun the powerful process of building a practice that can operate exactly as you expect it to.

By carefully thinking about exactly what to expect, you have already begun to improve your practice.

In this enlightened state, you will see the selection of your associ-ates as an opportunity to define what you (1) intend to provide for your clients, (2) expect from your employees, and (3) demand for your life.

Powerful stuff, isn't it? Are you up to it? Are you ready to feel your rising power?

Don't rest on your laurels just yet. Defining those standards is only the first step you need to take. The second step is to create an *associate financial advisor development system.*

An associate financial advisor development system is an action plan designed to tell you what you are looking for in an associate. It includes the exact benchmarks, accountabilities, timing of fulfill-ment, and budget you will assign to the process of looking for associate financial advisors, identifying them, recruiting them, inter-viewing them, training them, managing their work, auditing their performance, compensating them, reviewing them regularly, and terminating or rewarding them for their performance.

All of these things must be documented—actually *written down*—if they're going to make any difference to you, your associate financial advisors, your managers, or your bank account!

And then you've got to persist with that system, come hell or high water. Just as Ray Kroc did. Just as Walt Disney did. Just as Sam Walton did.

This leads us to our next topic of discussion: the subject of *estimating*. But first, let's listen to what Michael Steranka has to say on the subject of associate financial advisors. ✤

12

The Associate Financial Advisor

Michael Steranka

As we let our own light shine, we unconsciously give other people permission to do the same.
—Marianne Williamson, A Woman's Worth

Finding qualified associates can be one of the hardest challenges facing any successful professional services organization. It's no different for financial advisory firms.

As we discuss associates in this chapter, remember that in order to employ the right associates, you should already have established a personnel system that works for your business. With the proper systems in place, you'll know exactly what type of associates you need. You will be able to identify better what they're expected to do and what qualifications they must possess in order to meet those expectations.

Let's begin by asking, "What is an associate?"

An associate is somebody who is a planner in your office. One of your peers. He or she is someone you train to be another version of you, a representative of your firm.

I have one particular associate whom I want to introduce to you. This person is an exceptional young man named Brian Kuhn. He is a certified financial planner (CFP). Brian is well-groomed, polished, educated, and goal-driven. He has a thirst for knowledge and self-improvement greater than any other person I have ever worked with side-by-side. If I had ten Brian Kuhns, I would own the East Coast, if not the United States.

Although Brian is young in terms of age, he is old in spirit. He has the work ethic required of a true entrepreneur to become successful and stay successful, which is to say, he works as long as it takes to get the job done. Brian is "old school," meaning he actually works without looking to get paid for it. So many kids today want to waltz in and run the company. They demand six figures even when they can barely generate revenue. In our business, it's all about production and what you bring in. If you're bringing in a lot, then you're worth six figures. If you're not, you're worth $30,000, if even that.

Brian is incredibly thorough. He sits in on every one of my meetings and takes copious notes. I have created a coaching program and in that program, I've even carved out a niche called the "BK University," named for Brian. When I first hired Brian, somebody said, "Oh, you're going to love this kid." Brian came to me when I was quite busy. Sometimes, I was too busy to appreciate that he was right there every time I turned around, and I would simply dismiss him, sometimes unpleasantly. But after a while, I noticed that I was calling his name more and more frequently. Brian was and has become more valuable every day.

An associate like Brian is a rare find. He is the type of guy you'll feel comfortable turning your practice over to, an experienced and knowledgeable certified financial planner whom you can trust.

When you assess potential associates, make sure to look for well-rounded planners who possess important skill sets for every aspect of the business. Some knowledgeable people in our business can be a little dangerous because while they have knowledge, they have little-to-no clue about sales. These associates are professional information sources, but they can't close their way out of a paper bag. If you want to keep the lights on, you need to close. You need to retain clients and obtain new ones.

There are certain skill sets required for salesmanship that often go untaught or are neglected in most certified financial planning courses. I developed this skill set early on because I've been working ever since I was twelve years old. I had a paper route, and I was meeting the public all the time. At a very young age, I figured out that I liked dealing directly with other people. In sales, when you have a product or a service and you know that it can help a person out, you can offer that product or service, and if you position it correctly, that person will recognize that the sale is a win-win. The customer gets something and you get something.

Not only should you find associates who are knowledgeable and can sell, but you must find associates with whom you can work well and whom you can trust. When you're dealing with your livelihood and the livelihood of others, there's no such thing as being "too safe." I suggest drafting good agreements or contracts for the associates with whom you work. Include a noncompete clause, which states that your clients remain yours and that these associates cannot take your clients and/or your materials down the street to open up shop for themselves. You're bringing in millions of dollars and you need to protect your firm. Any respectful prospective employee, especially in a down economy, should have no problem signing a piece of paper to get hired to learn to make millions of dollars. In a slow economy, they should be thankful just to have a job.

As you hire associates, identify whether your prospects are people who you feel would represent your company well. The first impression they give to you is likely to be the first impression they'll give to clients. If someone dresses like a slob and talks like a slob, don't waste time giving him the benefit of the doubt. He is a slob. But if someone is well-dressed, well-spoken, polite, and educated, then he or she might be someone you want on your team. Look for people who have taken the initiative to pursue advanced training courses in the field. Look for people who remind you of yourself when you first started out.

When I first joined this industry, I did everything on my own. So I'm drawn to people who are also investing time, energy, and money in their careers even before getting hired. I see a little bit of myself in the other guys who say, "I've taken these two or three courses simply for my own benefit." They might be ten or fifteen years behind me, but the idea and work ethic are still the same. So identify what a potential associate looks like from an educational standpoint and then stand him up against what your company does and what your company needs.

I personally require all new hires to take the Kolbe Index, a survey that defines and assesses an individual's skill sets. I want to know where each person shines so he or she can be plugged into the proper role. We've even moved people around within our firm based on their Kolbe scores.

We've made only one new hire in the last two years, and this new hire first came in as a producer. On his Kolbe test, he scored really high on the Fact Finder and Follow Through, but low on the Quick Start. I find that most salesmen score pretty high on the Quick Start, so I was blunt with him and said, "I don't know that you're going to be a producer."

I told this new hire that he might want to be a producer, but from what I saw, everything about him says that he is someone who can push paper and perhaps push paper better than anybody in the world. I said, "This is where your specialty is and it's where you're most likely to find enjoyment and receive compensation." I think I surprised him a little bit, but it was better to lay the truth on him than to sugarcoat it.

In the past, when I didn't have those surveys, I oftentimes tried to push square pegs into round holes. Then I'd constantly be frustrated and ask why that person failed to do this or failed to do that when the answer was simply because that person *couldn't* do it. It wasn't in his DNA. His DNA made him better suited for another role at which he could excel.

The Kolbe tests are available at www.kolbc.com for a relatively low fee. I believe these tests are valuable because if you're going to invest time, energy, and money into a new hire, then you should find out how that person can be the most useful to your company.

Michael E. Gerber calls associates "technicians." These technicians are the people your firm needs in order to shine for your existing clients, your prospective clients, your strategic partners, and the community at large. You already set high standards for yourself. Make sure also to set high standards for potential associates, and you'll find yourself running a company of people who work as hard as you do.

Now let's find out what Michael E. Gerber has to say about estimating your fees. ✣

CHAPTER 13

On the Subject
of Estimating

Michael E. Gerber

The way a Chihuahua goes about eating a dead elephant is to take a bite and be very present with that bite. In spiritual growth, the definitive act is to take one step and let tomorrow's step take care of itself.
—William H. Houff, *Infinity in Your Hand: A Guide for the Spiritually Curious*

O ne of the greatest weaknesses of financial advisors is accurately estimating how long appointments will take and then scheduling their prospects and clients accordingly. *Webster's Eleventh Collegiate Dictionary* defines estimate as "a rough or approximate calculation." Anyone who has visited a financial advisor's lobby knows that those estimates can be rough indeed.

Do you want to see someone who gives you a rough approximation? What if your financial advisor gave you a rough approximation of your financial condition?

The fact is we can predict many things we don't typically predict. For example, there are ways to examine a client's portfolio and income needs and estimate how long her money will last. Look at the steps of the process. Most of the things you do are standard, so develop a step-by-step system and stick to it.

In my book *The E-Myth Manager*, I raised eyebrows by suggesting that the waiting room or lobby be eliminated. Why? You don't need it if you're always on time. The same goes for a financial advisory practice. If you're always on time, then your clients don't have to wait.

What if a financial advisor made this promise: On time, every time, as promised, or we pay for it.

"Impossible!" financial advisors cry. "Each client is different. We simply can't know how long each appointment will take."

Do you follow this? Since financial advisors believe they're incapable of knowing how to organize their time, they build a practice based on lack of knowing and lack of control. They build a practice based on estimates.

I once had a financial advisor ask me, "What happens when someone comes in for an annual review and we discover that their spouse passed away a month ago? How can we deal with someone so unexpected? How can we give proper advice and stay on schedule?" My first thought was that it's not being dealt with now. Few financial advisors are able to give generously of their time. Ask anyone who's been to a financial advisor's office lately. It's chaos.

The solution is interest, attention, analysis. Try detailing what you do at the beginning of an interaction, what you do in the middle, and what you do at the end. How long does each take? In the absence of such detailed, quantified standards, everything ends up being an estimate, and a poor estimate at that.

However, a practice organized around a system, with adequate staff to run it, has time for proper attention. It's built right into the system.

Too many financial advisors have grown accustomed to thinking in terms of estimates without thinking about what the term really means. Is it any wonder many financial advisory practices are in trouble?

Enlightened financial advisors, in contrast, banish the word *estimate* from their vocabulary. When it comes to estimating, just say "No"!

"But you can never be exact," financial advisors have told me for years. "Close, maybe. But never exact."

I have a simple answer to that: *You have to be.* You simply can't afford to be inexact. You can't accept inexactness in yourself or in your financial advisory practice.

You can't go to work every day believing that your practice, the work you do, and the commitments you make are all too complex and unpredictable to be exact. With a mindset like that, you're doomed to run a sloppy ship. A ship that will eventually sink and suck you down with it.

This is so easy to avoid. Sloppiness—in both thought and action—is the root cause of your frustrations.

The solution to those frustrations is clarity. Clarity gives you the ability to set a clear direction, which fuels the momentum you need to grow your business.

Clarity, direction, momentum—they all come from insisting on exactness.

But how do you create exactness in a hopelessly inexact world? The answer is: *You discover the exactness in your practice by refusing to do any work that can't be controlled exactly.*

The only other option is to analyze the market, determine where the opportunities are, and then organize your practice to be the exact provider of the services you've chosen to offer.

Two choices, and only two choices: (1) Evaluate your practice and then limit yourself to the tasks you know you can do exactly, or (2) start all over by analyzing the market, identifying the key opportunities in that market, and building a practice that operates exactly.

What you cannot do, what you must refuse to do, from this day forward, is to allow yourself to operate with an inexact mindset. It will lead you to ruin.

Which leads us inexorably back to the word I have been using through this book: *systems*.

Who makes estimates? Only financial advisors who are unclear about exactly how to do the task in question. Only financial advisors whose experience has taught them that if something can go wrong, it will—and to them!

I'm not suggesting that a *systems solution* will guarantee that you always perform exactly as promised. But I am saying that a systems solution will faithfully alert you when you're going off track, and will do it before you have to pay the price for it.

In short, with a systems solution in place, your need to estimate will be a thing of the past, both because you have organized your practice to anticipate mistakes, and because you have put into place the system to do something about those mistakes before they blow up.

There's this, too: To make a promise you intend to keep places a burden on you and your managers to dig deeply into how you intend to keep it. Such a burden will transform your intentions and increase your attention to detail.

With the promise will come dedication. With dedication will come integrity. With integrity will come consistency. With consistency will come results you can count on. And results you can count on mean that you get exactly what you hoped for at the outset of your practice: the true pride of ownership that every financial advisor should experience.

This brings us to the subject of *clients*. Who are they? Why do they come to you? How can you identify yours? And who *should* your clients be? But first, let's listen to what Michael Steranka has to say about estimating. ✤

CHAPTER 14

Billing and Certainty

Michael Steranka

Do not let what you cannot do interfere with what you can do.
—John Wooden

I s your business a brand new baby? Is it an ongoing concern—an established business—that has you running in place? No matter where in the curve you find yourself, this chapter will help you propel your business forward by addressing what it means to estimate and forecast properly.

The key with any estimate is to be entirely realistic and then shave the numbers back 30 percent or more. You can make any potential business look good on paper, but the real question is, can you achieve the results?

Let's first discuss the new "baby." How in the world do you start? Where do you start? What kind of funding do you need? Do you have the money at hand or do you need to borrow the money? Before you start fretting over these questions, begin at point zero. Identify exactly where you're standing. Ask yourself, "Where am I now? Am I even in business at all?"

Let's assume that you are so brand new that you haven't done a single thing for your business. In fact, you got your license today. Perhaps somebody somewhere recruited you and told you a compelling story about the financial advisory business. The story was compelling enough for you to go through all the necessary procedures and educational routes to become licensed. You took the test, passed it, and maybe now you're set up to begin working for the person who recruited you.

If you fit this description, then the odds are good that you are indeed working for that recruiter. The only problem is that the person you are working for may or may not have a viable system in place for you. In fact, most advisors don't. Most of them throw new guys and gals to the wolves and leave them to eat what they kill. If they survive, fantastic. If they don't, then maybe they should go back to their previous profession.

Chances are if you're a brand-new advisor, you may be working for the person who recruited you because he or she paid for your licensing. In fact, maybe that person paid for your office space, a receptionist, and some marketing materials, as well. In this case, that person most likely owns a fair percentage of your ongoing concern.

Even in this situation, I encourage you to create a game plan for the little enterprise that you are starting now. Dream big from the outset. On day one, immediately try to negotiate a plan through which you can fly away and do your own thing once you meet certain requirements. Come up with a strategy that eventually will allow you to take over the business you're working for. Do this right away; don't delay this type of planning.

If this business you've joined is ongoing and successful, it will require a large sum of money to acquire it. The reality is that you probably won't have that money for some time. But if you work your tail off for more than two, five, or ten years, you can make that money and build the experience and knowledge needed to master how the firm is operated, so much so that the owner will say, "Why don't you take over this business?" That's what you should be reaching for. That's where you ultimately want to go.

What if you're not completely new? Maybe you've been a financial planner for some time now, but you've just been in the business and you're not "in business." Perhaps you picked up this book because you're tired of simply wading in the financial advisory pool. You're no longer satisfied with just having a license. You're determined to start your own firm.

As I mentioned in the chapter on managing your company, the first thing you need to do is take an honest snapshot of what you're doing now. Make yourself do a harsh, but quick, reality check that determines where you currently are. I'll bet you're not making the money you want to make.

Some planners with new businesses sometimes do immediately make the money they intended to make. But then they lose themselves in a fantasy world in which that ideal income will always continue. And then when it doesn't continue, they pick up a book like this one.

If you're like those planners or you find yourself and your humble business at a standstill, the first thing to do is recognize that you have an issue or a problem that needs to be addressed. Then go back and assess how much money you actually generated over the last two years. Chart it out by month. Then chart your expenses and look at where your cash flow is and what you're doing to generate money.

I once went to a large life insurance company where I had to write a disability policy on the business owner. I paused at a section on the application that asked, "Does this business owner get more than 30 percent of his annual revenue in any one month?" I couldn't figure out how to answer this question. I didn't know whether answering "yes" or "no" was positive or negative, or whether this question was talking about seasonal businesses.

When I was in New York, I visited the company and found the chief underwriter in the disability department. I asked the underwriter, "What do you mean when you ask whether the owner generates 30 percent or more in a given month?"

He said, "Let me give you an example, Mike. Let's say you have a business owner and he makes $210,000 a year. Say he makes

$100,000 in January and then $10,000 a month for the rest of the year. We think that when this guy figures out his business, he has the potential to make $100,000 a month every month."

I was stunned. He continued, "We think that guy's got real potential. And if he stays in business, he'll probably figure out how to make $100,000 a month. So if anybody generates a large amount of revenue in a short period of time, all he or she has to do is figure out how to keep doing that."

Sounds simple enough, right? If you make a lot of money, figure out what you did right and then do that over and over again to continue making that much money. This is something I learned eighteen years ago. I've used it in my practice so we have brought in six figures every month for many years.

A lot of producers or advisors in our industry have a tendency to make a lot of money and then take time off, especially if they're brand new or somewhat new or just immature as business owners. These advisors will make $200,000 in one month and then think, "I'm sure I'll get another one like that." But there is no guarantee you'll get another deal like that. Instead, your thoughts should be redirected to how you *did* get that one and what you can do to replicate that. So instead of taking a premature break, the smart business move is to invest all your time, energy, and money into figuring out this pattern so you always have an opportunity to replicate that $200,000 a month. This is the type of planning, estimating, and forecasting required if you're serious about being in and staying in business.

Now let's say that you've been in business for a while, but you want to get to that next level. You attend meetings and conferences, see big producers, and wish you could be those people. I'll let you in on a secret: You already *are* those people. You just haven't applied your knowledge in the most efficient way yet, or you haven't acquired the same amount of knowledge as that bigger producer. But all the knowledge you'll ever need is always at hand.

I suggest approaching that big advisor to ask, "How in the world did you do this?" And then shut up and listen. Give that person an opportunity to give you some good tips on what you can do to grow your business.

In addition to asking bigger producers for advice, I suggest looking for a mentor. Find someone who is deriving the income that you want or has a practice that you admire. Then go to that person and say, "Hey, will you teach me?" If the answer is yes, that person might help you for free, but time is money, and most people cannot help you for free. Most planners will charge you something. Either they'll want you to write your business underneath them or through them, split work, or write them a separate check on a consulting basis.

The fee aside, this is the way you can supercharge things and get to levels that you want to get to faster than by trying to reinvent the wheel. And the fact is, in order to make money, you have to spend money. If you want to bring in $1 million a year in revenue, you'll probably have to spend even more. You may find yourself spending $250,000 to $500,000 at an absolute minimum. And many times, you'll spend substantially more than that.

You'll need to spend this much because you're not going to know what you're doing. You can plan on making many mistakes and getting frustrated. But when you have a mentor you can go back to, that person will be useful for when you need to say, "Look, I've got this problem. What do I do?" Or "I have this challenge. What do I do?" Or "I have this opportunity. What do I do with it?"

Over the years, I have attended workshops with people to whom I've paid substantial consulting fees. And sometimes, ten minutes into the two days of consulting, they'll give me one idea that gets me so excited that I want to leave the workshop right away to put that idea into practice. Once, I got an idea that literally brought in several hundred thousand dollars in revenue for a few years. I got that little idea from a consultant to whom I paid $20,000. But when you can get the type of return that I got from that consultant, $20,000 looks like a miniscule investment.

When you attend these conferences or workshops with hundreds of people and you see the same people receiving recognition every year for a job well done, don't be discouraged. I find that the temptation for most people is to chalk up those people's success to something like, "They have what it takes and I don't." This is simply untrue. Everyone can do it. Everyone can be that successful. Some just choose not to be.

This is a difficult truth to hear, but compare it to losing weight. If I eat potato chips every day, drink sugary soft drinks, and don't exercise, I can't be surprised when I don't lose weight. Some people get stuck in this rut and then look at someone who is losing weight and say, "It's easy for that person to lose weight. He's got a better metabolism than I do." Like those people, you have a choice: Are you going to make excuses or are you going to find a reason for why something isn't working?

When you are honest with yourself, you can estimate and forecast properly to reach your ultimate goal. Otherwise, you're being paid like one of the people you employ to do your paperwork, except you have worse headaches. For the same headaches, do you want a meager salary or do you want ten or twenty times that number? When you run your own business, the stress level will be the same. The headaches will be there. That's business. That's life. So why not compensate yourself twenty, thirty, or forty times more than what you're making now so those headaches will be well worth it?

Let's find out what Michael E. Gerber has to say about clients. ♣

CHAPTER

15

On the Subject
of Clients

Michael E. Gerber

Some patients I see are actually draining into their bodies the diseased
thoughts of their minds.
  —Zachary T. Bercovitz, *Wisdom for the Soul: Five Millennia of*
Prescriptions for Spiritual Healing

W hen it comes to the practice of financial advisory, the best
definition of clients I've ever heard is this:

Clients: very special people who drive most financial advisors crazy.
Does that work for you? After all, it's a rare client who shows
any appreciation for what a financial advisor has to go through to
do the job as promised. Don't they always think the price is too
high? And don't they focus on problems, broken promises, and the
mistakes they think you make, rather than all the ways you bend
over backward to give them what they need?

Do you ever hear other financial advisors voice these complaints?
More to the point, have you ever voiced them yourself? Well, you're

not alone. I have yet to meet a financial advisor who doesn't suffer from a strong case of client confusion.

Client confusion is about

- what your client really wants;
- how to communicate effectively with your client;
- how to keep your client happy;
- how to deal with client dissatisfaction; and
- whom to call a client.

Confusion 1: What Your Client Really Wants

Your clients aren't just people; they're very specific kinds of people. Let me share with you the six categories of clients as seen from the E-Myth marketing perspective: (1) tactile clients, (2) neutral clients, (3) withdrawal clients, (4) experimental clients, (5) transitional clients, and (6) traditional clients.

Your entire marketing strategy must be based on which type of client you are dealing with. Each of the six client types spends money on financial advisory services for very different, and identifiable, reasons. These are:

- Tactile clients get their major gratification from interacting with other people.
- Neutral clients get their major gratification from interacting with inanimate objects (computers, cars, information).
- Withdrawal clients get their major gratification from interacting with ideas (thoughts, concepts, stories).
- Experimental clients rationalize their buying decisions by perceiving that what they bought is new, revolutionary, and innovative.
- Transitional clients rationalize their buying decisions by perceiving that what they bought is dependable and reliable.
- Traditional clients rationalize their buying decisions by perceiving that what they bought is cost-effective, a good deal, and worth the money.

In short:

- If your client is tactile, you have to emphasize the *people* of your practice.
- If your client is neutral, you have to emphasize the *technology* of your practice.
- If your client is a withdrawal client, you have to emphasize the *idea* of your practice.
- If your client is experimental, you have to emphasize the *uniqueness* of your practice.
- If your client is transitional, you have to emphasize the *dependability* of your practice.
- If your client is traditional, you have to talk about the *financial competitiveness* of your practice.

What your clients want is determined by who they are. Who they are is regularly demonstrated by what they do. Think about the clients with whom you do business. Ask yourself: In which of the categories would I place them? What do they do for a living?

If your client is a mechanical engineer, for example, it's probably safe to assume he's a neutral client. If another one of your clients is a cardiologist, she's probably tactile. Accountants tend to be traditional, and software engineers are often experimental.

Having an idea about which categories your clients may fall into is very helpful to figuring out what they want. Of course, there's no exact science to it, and human beings constantly defy stereotypes. So don't take my word for it. You'll want to make your own analysis of the clients you serve.

Confusion 2: How to Communicate Effectively with Your Client

The next step in the client-satisfaction process is to decide how to magnify the characteristics of your practice that are most likely to appeal to your preferred category of client. That begins with what marketing people call your *positioning strategy*.

What do I mean by *positioning* your practice? You position your practice with words. A few well-chosen words to tell your clients exactly what they want to hear. In marketing lingo, those words are called your USP, or unique selling proposition.

For example, if you are targeting tactile clients (ones who love people), your USP could be: "Premier Financial Solutions, where the feelings of people *really* count!"

If you are targeting experimental clients (ones who love new, revolutionary things), your USP could be: "Premier Financial Solutions, where living on the edge is a way of life!" In other words, when they choose to schedule an appointment with you, they can count on both your services and software to be on the cutting edge of the financial advisory industry.

Is this starting to make sense? Do you see how the ordinary things most financial advisors do to get clients can be done in a significantly more effective way?

Once you understand the essential principles of marketing the E-Myth way, the strategies by which you attract clients can make an enormous difference in your market share.

Confusion 3: How to Keep Your Client Happy

Let's say you've overcome the first three confusions. Great. Now how do you keep your client happy?

Very simple . . . just keep your promise! And make sure your client *knows* you kept your promise every step of the way.

In short, giving your clients what they think they want is the key to keeping your clients (or anyone else, for that matter) really happy.

If your clients need to interact with people (high touch, tactile), make certain that they do.

If they need to interact with things (high-tech, neutral), make certain that they do.

If they need to interact with ideas (in their head, withdrawal), make certain that they do.

And so forth.

At E-Myth, we call this your *client fulfillment system.* It's the step-by-step process by which you do the task you've contracted to do and deliver what you've promised—on time, every time.

But what happens when your clients are *not* happy? What happens when you've done everything I've mentioned here and your client is still dissatisfied?

Confusion 4: How to Deal with Client Dissatisfaction

If you have followed each step up to this point, client dissatisfaction will be rare. But it can and will still occur—people are people, and some people will always find a way to be dissatisfied with something. Here's what to do about it:

- Always listen to what your clients are saying. And never interrupt while they're saying it.
- After you're sure you've heard all of your client's concern, make absolutely certain you understand what she said by phrasing a question, such as: "Can I repeat what you've just told me, Ms. Harton, to make absolutely certain I understand you?"
- Secure your client's acknowledgment that you have heard her complaint accurately.
- Apologize for whatever your client thinks you did that dissatisfied her, even if you didn't do it!
- After your client has acknowledged your apology, ask her exactly what would make her happy.
- Repeat what your client told you would make her happy, and get her acknowledgment that you have heard correctly.
- If at all possible, give your client exactly what she has asked for.
- You may be thinking, "But what if my client wants something totally impossible?" Don't worry. If you've followed my recommendations to the letter, what your client asks for will seldom seem unreasonable.

Confusion 5: Whom to Call a Client

At this stage, it's important to ask yourself some questions about the kind of clients you hope to attract to your practice:

- Which types of clients would you most like to do business with?
- Where do you see your real market opportunities?
- Who would you like to work with, provide services to, and position your business for?

To what category of client are you most drawn? A tactile client for whom people are most important? A neutral client for whom the mechanics of how you practice financial advisory is most important? An experimental client for whom cutting-edge innovation is important? A traditional client for whom low cost and certainty of delivery are absolutely essential?

Once you've defined your ideal clients, go after them. There's no reason you can't attract these types of people to your practice and give them exactly what they want.

In short, *it's all up to you.* No mystery. No magic. Just a systematic process for shaping your practice's future. But you must have the passion to pursue the process. And you must be absolutely clear about every aspect of it.

Until you know your clients as well as you know yourself.

Until all your complaints about clients are a thing of the past.

Until you accept the undeniable fact that client acquisition and client satisfaction are more science than art.

But unless you're willing to grow your practice, you better not follow any of these recommendations. Because if you do what I'm suggesting, it's going to grow.

This brings us to the subject of *growth*. But first, let's listen to what Michael Steranka has to say about clients. ✤

Your Clients Love You, They Love You Not

Michael Steranka

You may only be someone in the world, but to someone else, you may be the world.

—Source unknown

C lients are the reason we do what we do. If you ever reach a point where you don't care about your clients, then it's time to leave the business or reassess your practice. I have met many fine financial advisors who seemed to be at odds with their clients, but upon self-reflection, they realized that they were actually at odds with their own processes or lack thereof.

I truly love my clients. I have invited them to my home. I have taken them on field trips to New York City. I've hosted numerous cookouts and luaus to show my appreciation. In this chapter, I'll dive deeper into what it means to be the type of financial advisor who truly serves the client.

Let me tell you what I mean when I say that I love my clients. I consider my clients an extension of my family. I don't settle for only improving their situations, but also improving the lives of my clients' children and grandchildren as well.

Being a financial advisor is like being a doctor—a money doctor. Plus, you're able to fix a client financially for potentially two or three generations. And having that kind of impact on your client and your client's entire family is not only phenomenal; it can also be extremely rewarding.

There are several different types of clients. Some clients will do everything you suggest because they trust you 100 percent. Other clients will do most of what you suggest. Then you'll have a few who will do very little of what you suggest. I generally try to do business with the first two types.

The clients who take only a small percentage of your recommendations don't really value your opinion and are too restricted by their need for control. Some people even rebuff ideas simply because they didn't come up with those ideas themselves. As these types of clients age and recognize their own mortality, some of them eventually turn into more open, teachable clients. But I prefer doing business with people who will take my recommendations.

Of course, I don't expect my clients to buy into 100 percent of what I suggest from day one. That kind of trust takes years to build. Occasionally, a client will trust me immediately because he or she had a strong referral from somebody who already knows me.

I've had certain clients who were extremely thorough and meticulous in the planning process. In fact, they were so thorough that when they referred me to other people, those people came in, laid everything down and said, "Look, if you can deal with Charlie after what he puts everybody through, you're good enough for us."

Our firm doesn't take everybody on as a client. I review the prospective client files with three or four members of my staff to decide whether we want to take each prospect as a client. If we took everybody on, we could make more money, but we'd have more headaches! So we consider whose personalities will mesh with ours and whether they will be open to our advice and recommendations. I have been in situations in which I'm trying to help a client do something that will save him millions of dollars in taxes, yet he struggles with the decision. He may even be suspicious or hesitant.

Then there are others who've gotten by for a fair amount of time managing their own money. But eventually, even the smartest people have to consult a professional. Sure, they could create a last will and testament with a form from their local Staples, but it may not be valid in all fifty states. Sometimes attempting to do something like that is like acting as your own attorney in court, or worse, like being your own brain surgeon.

The purpose of a financial advisor is to give clients expert advice in specific areas of their financial lives. We pinpoint specific areas of need and then figure out what recommendations to make or which specialists they should see.

And here's an interesting fact: I've often found that the person who has a small net worth generally doesn't trust people or take advice from others. Maybe that person is worried about losing what he has. But his net worth is not going to grow unless he heeds the advice of an experienced planner like me.

I may deal with a number of different clients, but the service I provide is the same across the board. The question I pound home with my staff and my clients is: "What additional services can we bring to the table?" This is how we determine whether to have more guest speaker events or another holiday event with an eight-piece orchestra, open bar, and gaming tables.

We even poll our clients about their favorite types of activities. In one year, we sponsored ten events, from wine tastings to a cooking class to a dancing class, as opportunities for our clients to interact with each other and with our staff in a nonfinancial setting.

My clients teach me new things every day. They may not teach me something related to money, but they always teach me something about life. As we discover our clients' passions, our own passions begin to expand. One of our clients has a strong commitment to the local opera. So now we're helping to support local arts.

If we have a client who is passionate about a cause in the community, a church, or an institution, we brainstorm ways to help the client make a large donation. We save our clients' money in taxes while providing funds, ranging from several thousands to several millions of dollars, to that nonprofit group. The clients like it. The group likes it. It's a win-win for everybody. But in order to do this, we must first get to know our clients on a personal level.

It's crucial to answer the phone and be in the office during business hours so you're available to the client. I have picked up many accounts from people who have said that their previous advisor was never available. Today, the business model of the up-and-coming e-trades and online transactions is not founded in service. These businesses are unabashedly about getting as many people as they can to buy their products.

In an era in which online trading has become a pervasive form of investing, too many newer brokers don't have a service mentality as they interact with their clients. The companies that they're most accustomed to hearing about or dealing with or using themselves are not about service. If you call one of these businesses and ask for advice, they won't give you any because that's not what they're getting paid to do. They might have added a separate division that does tell you what to do, but in order to access that division, you have to pay a fee.

The only model I know of that supports the type of services that most people want as it relates to their financial planning at or near retirement is a true, independent advisor who can move as the clients move. I have some clients who only have CDs, tax-exempt bonds, and some fixed annuities. That's a package you won't get at a "wire house" because they can't make any money from it.

But maybe the days of making money off that type of client are over. The right thing to do is to service those clients and make sure they receive income for the rest of their lives. Then when they leave their money to their kids, you'll get a chance to keep that money in house because you took care of the parents.

Constantly looking for the next transaction is a poor business model for advisory firms. Transactions will come as life events occur, but you can't force those transactions on your clients. They'll make their own rational decisions in their own time, based on the information you give them.

Treat your clients with integrity and patience, and you'll be sure to retain them and also gain valuable referrals. The surest way to be successful in this business is to be less concerned about your money and more considerate of what your clients should do with theirs.

Now let's consider Michael E. Gerber's thoughts about growth. ✤

On the Subject of Growth

Michael E. Gerber

Growth is the only evidence of life.
    —John Henry Newman, *Apologia Pro Vita Sua*

The rule of business growth says that every business, like every child, is destined to grow. Needs to grow. Is determined to grow.

Once you've created your financial advisory practice, once you've shaped the idea of it, the most natural thing for it to do is to . . . *grow!* And if you stop it from growing, it will die.

Once a financial advisor has started a practice, it's his or her job to help it grow. To nurture it and support it in every way. To infuse it with these qualities:

- Purpose
- Passion
- Will
- Belief

- Personality
- Method

As your practice grows, it naturally changes. And as it changes from a small practice to something much bigger, you will begin to feel out of control. News flash: That's because you *are* out of control.

Your practice *has* exceeded your know-how, sprinted right past you, and now it's taunting you to keep up. That leaves you two choices: Grow as big as your practice demands you grow, or try to hold your practice at its present level—at the level you feel most comfortable.

The sad fact is that most financial advisors do the latter. They try to keep their practice small, securely within their comfort zone. Doing what they know how to do, what they feel most comfortable doing. It's called playing it safe.

But as the practice grows, the number, scale, and complexity of tasks will grow, too, until they threaten to overwhelm the financial advisor. More people are needed. More space. More money. Everything seems to be happening at the same time. A hundred balls are in the air at once.

As I've said throughout this book: *Most financial advisors are not entrepreneurs. They aren't true businesspeople at all, but technicians suffering from an entrepreneurial seizure.* Their philosophy of coping with the workload can be summarized as "just do it," rather than figuring out how to get it done through other people using innovative systems to produce consistent results.

Given most financial advisors' inclination to be the master juggler in their practice, it's not surprising that as complexity increases, as work expands beyond their ability to do it, as money becomes more elusive, they are just holding on, desperately juggling more and more balls. In the end, most collapse under the strain.

You can't expect your practice to stand still. You can't expect your practice to stay small. A practice that stays small and depends on you to do everything isn't a practice—it's a job!

Yes, just like your children, your business must be allowed to grow, to flourish, to change, to become more than it is. In this way, it will match your vision. And you know all about vision, right? You better. It's what you do best!

Do you feel the excitement? You should. After all, you know what your practice *is* but not what it *can be*.

It's either going to grow or die. The choice is yours, but it is a choice that must be made. If you sit back and wait for change to overtake you, you will always have to answer no to this question: Are you ready?

This brings us to the subject of *change*. But first, let's listen to what Michael Steranka has to say about growth. ✤

Growing Joys

Michael Steranka

If we're growing, we're always going to be out of our comfort zone.
—John Maxwell

Now that we've covered the systems your business requires as well as the people who can work within the systems and the people those systems should serve, let's talk seriously about growth.

Managing growth is much more complicated than . . . managing growth. It requires managing everything we've discussed, from expectations, budgets, and forecasts to office personnel and associates to a million other little things that pop up when you least expect them.

But before you can manage growth, you need to identify what growth means to you and your business. Where do you ultimately want to go and how is that place different from where you are now? Is your ultimate goal to build the business and sell it? Or are you happy just squeaking by and making a living? I would personally want to make as much money as I can as quickly as I can and then sell the business for profit.

I often meet with my accountant and make large deposits in the bank. I would like for my firm's growth to include more of those large deposits. What I consider large deposits will be different from yours or somebody else's. But it is important for me to determine exactly how large I want those deposits to be and how often I want to make them.

For example, to really hit my ultimate goal, I imagine I'd have to make approximately forty more large deposits. Once I decide on the numbers I want to meet, I can then map out how I will get there. But depositing large checks isn't everybody's idea of growth. So your first step is to reflect and determine what you want out of your business. Your ultimate business goal will dictate what kind of growth and how much growth you'll want to try to achieve.

Even when you know exactly where you want to go, growth occurs in stages and sometimes in spurts. Even as your business grows, life happens, meaning sometimes you make good decisions and sometimes you make poor decisions. Sometimes other people's poor decisions also affect you. Managing growth involves dealing with the fallout of some of those decisions. Hopefully, you'll have mentors in place and others you can trust to give you constructive feedback so that you don't repeat those mistakes.

If you are a financial planner who has been successful in your business but are frustrated because you're "doing it, doing it, doing it," as Michael E. Gerber says, and you want to reach that next level, then managing growth boils down to your systems. Without a proper system in place for your business—without a well-thought-out, written-down plan—you don't stand a chance. If you don't know where you're going, how will you know which roads to take and whether you got there?

An unnerving number of businesspeople march forward with no plan or system in place. But if you're prepared and you do have your system, then you can measure it so all you need to do is tweak it from time to time when something fails to work. When things go wrong, instead of scrambling to create or establish last-minute systems, you can make adjustments on the ones that exist.

Perhaps your business has been growing because you've managed yourself well. You've got the "me" part handled. You're talented, you're a little lucky, you can sell, and you're diligent. But what about the business as a business? Growth management doesn't actually start with you. It starts with the details of your systems, which give you the measurable results you need to monitor how you are meeting your goals. To allow your systems to help your business grow efficiently, you have to learn to remove yourself from the equation.

Most advisors can't get out of their own way. They overinflate their work. They believe that they're more valuable than they actually are. This isn't to say that they're not valuable. They are. But the point is that just because they're valuable doesn't mean they have to do the job themselves. Somebody else in the firm may be as capable or even more capable at accomplishing certain functions.

If you're tied up in all the little details, you will never be able to grow. You need others to handle the basic operations so you can do something else. When I recommend this to some advisors, they justify taking on these smaller jobs by saying that they're the only ones qualified. This may well be true, but there are even more important tasks that need their attention.

If you want your business to grow, you have to learn to let go of parts of your business and not micromanage everything. You have to relinquish control to other people on your staff who are capable and trust them to get the job done.

Remember that you have your systems in place so you can easily monitor whether everything is being accomplished. Instead of micromanaging the details, you'll monitor the bigger picture and give yourself room to grow. This is when growth can really go off the charts because you'll actually have time to look at what could bring in more revenue to the company.

As you make plans and estimations for growth, I suggest planning generally for one year at a time. I have some longer-range plans, but most of them are a year out. You can certainly make plans as far as three or five years out, but I guarantee that something will change during that three to five years. If you make plans for a year, you won't have to make as many adjustments as things change. And no matter how well you plan for growth, your plans and your business will change.

Some systems will work and others won't. If they don't, you'll have to figure out why and what you can do about it. Two important keys to growth are remaining flexible and adapting well to change.

Being flexible also means being open to more growth than you anticipated. Don't be afraid to dream big. Set big goals and hire an excellent staff to help you reach those goals.

Someone once told me that I could never exceed $30 million in annual sales because it was simply too much paperwork. But I imagined that I could hire more people and train them on the systems in order to do substantially more business.

That conversation took place about six years ago and since then, my average production has greatly exceeded $30 million. Had I listened to my mentor and stopped at $30 million a year in sales, I would have lost approximately $4.5 million in fees and commissions by now. That's a lot of lost revenue.

Preparing yourself for growth involves preparing yourself for the ebb and flow of business. The economy is fickle. The market will go up, and sometimes it'll go down. But no matter what curveballs come your way, face them, deal with them, and even be glad to have them. Don't be discouraged and keep moving forward even when you feel this growth stretches you.

Some people remain satisfied with staying in one place, just sticking with what they know. But I have a feeling you're not "some people." You're someone who wants to keep growing. So grow. Let yourself stretch until your business finally reaches its ultimate destination.

In the next chapter, Michael E. Gerber shares his thoughts about change. ✦

On the Subject of Change

Michael E. Gerber

There is nothing permanent except change.
—Heraclitus of Ephesus, *Lives of the Philosophers*

So your practice is growing. That means, of course, that it's also changing. Which means it's driving you and everyone in your life crazy.

That's because, to most people, change is a diabolical thing. Tell most people they've got to change, and their first instinct is to crawl into a hole. Nothing threatens their existence more than change. Nothing cements their resistance more than change. Nothing.

Yet for the past thirty-five years, that's exactly what I've been proposing to small business owners: the need to change. Not for the sake of change itself, but for the sake of their lives.

I've talked to countless financial advisors whose hopes weren't being realized through their practice; whose lives were consumed by work; who slaved increasingly longer hours for decreasing pay; whose dissatisfaction grew as their enjoyment shriveled; whose practice had become the worst job in the world; whose money was out of control; whose employees were a source of never-ending hassles, just like their clients, their bank, and, increasingly, even their family.

More and more, these financial advisors spent their time alone, dreading the unknown and anxious about the future. And even when they were with people, they didn't know how to relax. Their mind was always on the job. They were distracted by work, by the thought of work. By the fear of falling behind.

And yet, when confronted with their condition and offered an alternative, most of the same financial advisors strenuously resisted. They assumed that if there were a better way of doing business, they already would have figured it out. They derived comfort from knowing what they believed they already knew. They accepted the limitations of being a financial advisor; or the truth about people; or the limitations of what they could expect from their clients, their employees, their associate financial advisors, their bankers—even their family and friends.

In short, most financial advisors I've met over the years would rather live with the frustrations they already have than risk enduring new frustrations.

Isn't that true of most people you know? Rather than opening up to the infinite number of possibilities life offers, they prefer to shut their life down to respectable limits. After all, isn't that the most reasonable way to live?

I think not. I think we must learn to let go. I think that if you fail to embrace change, it will inevitably destroy you.

Conversely, by opening yourself to change, you give your financial advisory practice the opportunity to get the most from your talents.

Let me share with you an original way to think about change, about life, about who we are and what we do. About the stunning notion of expansion and contraction.

Contraction versus Expansion

"Our salvation," a wise man once said, "is to allow." That is, to be open, to let go of our beliefs, to change. Only then can we move from a point of view to a viewing point.

That wise man was Thaddeus Golas, the author of a small, powerful book entitled *The Lazy Man's Guide to Enlightenment* (Seed Center, 1971).

Among the many inspirational things he had to say was this compelling idea:

The basic function of each being is expanding and contracting. Expanded beings are permeative; contracted beings are dense and impermeative. Therefore each of us, alone or in combination, may appear as space, energy, or mass, depending on the ratio of expansion to contraction chosen, and what kind of vibrations each of us expresses by alternating expansion and contraction. Each being controls his [or her] own vibrations.

In other words, Golas tells us that the entire mystery of life can be summed up in two words: *expansion* and *contraction*. He goes on to say:

We experience expansion as awareness, comprehension, understanding, or whatever we wish to call it.

When we are completely expanded, we have a feeling of total awareness, of being one with all life.

At that level we have no resistance to any vibrations or inter-actions of other beings. It is timeless bliss, with unlimited choice of consciousness, perception, and feeling.

When a (human) being is totally contracted, he is a mass particle, completely imploded.

To the degree that he is contracted, a being is unable to be in the same space with others, so the contraction is felt as fear, pain, unconsciousness, ignorance, hatred, evil, and a whole host of strange feelings.

At an extreme (of contraction, a human being) has the feeling of being completely insane, of resisting everyone and everything, of being unable to choose the content of his consciousness.

Of course, these are just the feelings appropriate to mass vibration levels, and he can get out of them at any time by expanding, by letting go of all resistance to what he thinks, sees, or feels.

Stay with me here. Because what Golas says is profoundly important. When you're feeling oppressed, overwhelmed, exhausted by more than you can control—contracted, as Golas puts it—you can change your state to one of expansion.

According to Golas, the more contracted we are, the more threatened we are by change; the more expanded we are, the more open we are to change.

In our most enlightened—that is, open—state, change is as welcome as non-change. Everything is perceived as a part of ourselves. There is no inside or outside. Everything is one thing. Our sense of isolation is transformed to a feeling of ease, of light, of joyful relationship with everything.

As infants, we didn't even think of change in the same way, because we lived those first days in an unthreatened state. Insensitive to the threat of loss, most young children are only aware of *what is.* Change is simply another form of *what is.* Change just *is.*

However, when we are in our most contracted—that is, closed— state, change is the most extreme threat. If the known is what I have, then the unknown must be what threatens to take away what I have. Change, then, is the unknown. And the unknown is fear. It's like being between trapezes.

- To the fearful, change is threatening because things may get worse.
- To the hopeful, change is encouraging because things may get better.
- To the confident, change is inspiring because the challenge exists to improve things.

If you are fearful, you see difficulties in every opportunity. If you are fear-free, you see opportunities in every difficulty.

Fear protects what I have from being taken away. But it also disconnects me from the rest of the world. In other words, fear keeps me separate and alone.

Here's the exciting part of Golas's message: With this new understanding of contraction and expansion, we can become completely attuned to where we are at all times.

If I am afraid, suspicious, skeptical, and resistant, I am in a contracted state. If I am joyful, open, interested, and willing, I am in an expanded state. Just knowing this puts me on an expanded path. Always remembering this, Golas says, brings enlightenment, which opens me even more.

Such openness gives me the ability to freely access my options. And taking advantage of options is the best part of change. Just as there are infinite ways to greet a client, there are infinite ways to run your practice. If you believe Thaddeus Golas, your most exciting option is to be open to all of them.

Because your life is lived on a continuum between the most contracted and most expanded—the most closed and most open—states, change is best understood as the movement from one to the other, and back again.

Most small business owners I've met see change as a thing in itself, as something that just happens to them. Most experience change as a threat. Whenever change shows up at the door, they quickly slam it. Many bolt the door and pile up the furniture. Some even run for their gun.

Few of them understand that change isn't a thing in itself, but rather the manifestation of many things. You might call it the revelation of all possibilities. Think of it as the ability at any moment to sacrifice what we are for what we could become.

Change can either challenge us or threaten us. It's our choice. Our attitude toward change can either pave the way to success or throw up a roadblock.

Change is where opportunity lives. Without change we would stay exactly as we are. The universe would be frozen still. Time would end.

At any given moment, we are somewhere on the path between a contracted and expanded state. Most of us are in the middle of the journey, neither totally closed nor totally open. According to Golas, change is our movement from one place in the middle toward one of the two ends.

Do you want to move toward contraction or toward enlightenment? Because without change, you are hopelessly stuck with what you've got.

Without change,

- we have no hope;
- we cannot know true joy;
- we will not get better; and
- we will continue to focus exclusively on what we have and the threat of losing it.

All of this negativity contracts us even more, until, at the extreme closed end of the spectrum, we become a black hole so dense that no light can escape.

Sadly, the harder we try to hold on to what we've got, the less able we are to do so. So we try still harder, which eventually drags us even deeper into the black hole of contraction.

Are you like that? Do you know anybody who is?

Think of change as the movement between where we are and where we're not. That leaves only two directions for change: either moving forward or slipping backward. We become either more contracted or more expanded.

The next step is to link change to how we feel. If we feel afraid, change is dragging us backward. If we feel open, change is pushing us forward.

Change is not a thing in itself, but a movement of our consciousness. By tuning in, by paying attention, we get clues to the state of our being.

Change, then, is not an outcome or something to be acquired. Change is a shift of our consciousness, of our being, of our humanity, of our attention, of our relationship with all other beings in the universe.

We are either "more in relationship" or "less in relationship." Change is the movement in either of those directions. The exciting part is that *we possess the ability to decide which way we go . . . and to know in the moment which way we're moving.*

Closed, open. . . . Open, closed. Two directions in the universe. The choice is yours.

Do you see the profound opportunity available to you? What an extraordinary way to live!

Enlightenment is not reserved for the sainted. Rather, it comes to us as we become more sensitive to ourselves. Eventually, we become our own guides, alerting ourselves to our state, moment by moment: *open . . . closed . . . open . . . closed.*

Listen to your inner voice, your ally, and feel what it's like to be open and closed. Experience the instant of choice in both directions.

You will feel the awareness growing. It may be only a flash at first, so be alert. This feeling is accessible, but only if you avoid the black hole of contraction.

Are you afraid that you're totally contracted? Don't be—it's doubtful. The fact that you're still reading this book suggests that you're moving in the opposite direction.

You're more like a running back seeking the open field. You can see the opportunity gleaming in the distance. In the open direction.

Understand that I'm not saying that change itself is a point on the path; rather, it's the all-important movement.

Change is *in you,* not *out there.*

What path are you on? The path of liberation? Or the path of crystallization?

As we know, change can be for the better or for the worse.

If change is happening inside of you, it is for the worse only if you remain closed to it. The key, then, is your attitude—your acceptance or rejection of change. Change can be for the better only if you accept it. And it will certainly be for the worse if you don't.

Remember, change is nothing in itself. Without you, change doesn't exist. Change is happening inside of each of us, giving us clues to where we are at any point in time.

Rejoice in change, for it's a sign you are alive.

Are we open? Are we closed? If we're open, good things are bound to happen. If we're closed, things will only get worse.

According to Golas, it's as simple as that. Whatever happens defines where we are. *How* we are is *where* we are. It cannot be any other way.

For change is life.

Charles Darwin wrote, "It is not the strongest of the species that survive, nor the most intelligent, but the one that proves itself most responsive to change."

The growth of your financial advisory practice, then, is its change. Your role is to go with it, to be with it, to share the joy, embrace the opportunities, meet the challenges, learn the lessons.

Remember, there are three kinds of people: (1) those who make things happen, (2) those who let things happen, and (3) those who wonder what the hell happened. The people who make things happen are masters of change. The other two are its victims.

Which type are you?

The Big Change

If all this is going to mean anything to the life of your practice, you have to know when you're going to leave it. At what point, in your practice's rise from where it is now to where it can ultimately grow, are you going to sell it? Because if you don't have a clear picture of when you want out, your practice is the master of your destiny, not the reverse.

As we stated earlier, the most valuable form of money is equity, and unless your business vision includes your equity and how you will use it to your advantage, you will forever be consumed by your practice.

Your practice is potentially the best friend you ever had. It is your practice's nature to serve you, so let it. If, however, you are not a wise steward, if you do not tell your practice what you expect from it, it will run rampant, abuse you, use you, and confuse you.

Change. Growth. Equity.

Focus on the point in the future when you will take leave of your practice. Now reconsider your goals in that context. Be specific. Write them down.

Skipping this step is like tiptoeing through earthquake country. Who can say where the fault line is waiting? And who knows exactly when your whole world may come crashing down around you?

Which brings us to the subject of time. But first, let's listen to what Michael Steranka has to say about change. ❧

The Gift of Change

Michael Steranka

The fact is that five years ago . . . I, as I am now, didn't exist at all.
Will the same thing happen in the next five years? I hope so.
— Siegfried Sassoon

Dan Sullivan, co-founder of Strategic Coach, wrote that if we're really growing, then in five years, we will not be doing the same job we're doing now. Ideally, we should be changing or evolving every five years. This doesn't mean that we have to undergo a wholesale change. I don't mean that we should change careers or industries. But the service or function we provide within our industry can change.

In an earlier chapter, we discussed that it is important to be flexible to help your business grow. In this chapter, we'll see that in order to grow, you also have to be open to change.

In the field of finance, if you're not open to adapting and changing to the circumstances around you, your business will quickly die. This is especially true with keeping up to date with technology. With all the new advances in technology, who knows what the next new phenomenon will be. The way I interact with clients has changed in countless ways over the span of my career. I can only imagine the way technology will continue to revolutionize our industry and our relationships with our clients.

When I first entered the business, we didn't even have personal computers. In order to get a life insurance quote, I had to read a table. There was one central computer for our entire office, so if I wanted to find a quote without looking it up manually, that super-computer could figure it out for me. Eventually, I purchased my first laptop–a 386 SX computer that weighed almost twelve pounds. It had a dot matrix printer, and I thought I was on fire!

I envision a time not even too long from now when we will probably be able to have clients in every state. Through online video programs like Skype, advisors can communicate with clients from almost anywhere. Of course, you might need representatives to visit the clients to secure proper documentation, notarize papers, guarantee signatures, and so forth, but the days of having to be in front of somebody physically may almost be over.

As communications and technology change, you will need to alter your business practices accordingly. You should also expect that your clients will change. Some clients even modify their spending habits over time. As a financial advisor, it is important to understand the aging process of consumers and how this process affects their expectations and needs. Your client will continually learn, grow, and evolve as a whole person, and so should you. The more I am able to develop as a whole person myself, the better equipped I am to be of service to my clients.

As I grow in my business and gain more knowledge, sometimes I even decide that I'm better suited for something I hadn't imagined I would do. At other times, I figure out that the position that I have been tied to for years is actually better left to somebody else in my office.

You will never know what talents your people have until you step out of the way and give them the opportunity to prove themselves.

As you practice this, not only will you see your staff change, but you and your business will also improve for the better.

I understand that by picking up this book, you're already an above-average businessperson. You're out there and you've survived that initial cut of the 90 percent to 95 percent of people who wash out in the first three years. You're well aware that change happens and will continue to happen. But even the most sophisticated people in the industry sometimes have an aversion to change, sometimes without realizing it.

It's fine if I want to pull out the books and figure out an insurance quote by hand. But if that old-fashioned way is my preference, I'd at least better be aware that I have the option of pressing a button on the computer to get the answer in one second as opposed to five or ten minutes. If I'm not aware of it, chances are my competitors are aware of it, and I'll look pretty foolish to my clients if they mention something and I say I have no idea what they're talking about.

Some clients don't like change and they like things done a certain way. But it's your job as a financial advisor at least to bring them into the twenty-first century and show them what's available. In order to do that, you have to study these changes and new offerings first.

The more willing you are to accept the changes occurring around you, the better and faster you will adapt, and the easier it will be to keep your business in pace with the world.

We have a few more pixels to put in place, so let's see what Michael E. Gerber has to say about time. ♣

CHAPTER
21

On the Subject
of Time

Michael E. Gerber

*Take time to deliberate; but when the time for action arrives, stop
thinking and go in.*

—Andrew Jackson

"I'm running out of time!" financial advisors often lament.
"I've got to learn how to manage my time more carefully!"

Of course, they see no real solution to this problem.
They're just worrying the subject to death. Singing the financial
advisor's blues.

Some make a real effort to control time. Maybe they go to time
management classes, or faithfully try to record their activities during
every hour of the day.

But it's hopeless. Even when financial advisors work harder,
even when they keep precise records of their time, there's always a
shortage of it. It's as if they're looking at a square clock in a round
universe. Something doesn't fit. The result: The financial advisor is
constantly chasing work, money, life.

And the reason is simple. Financial advisors don't see time for what it really is. They think of time with a small "t," rather than Time with a capital "T."

Yet Time is simply another word for *your life*. It's your ultimate asset, your gift at birth—and you can spend it any way you want. Do you know how you want to spend it? Do you have a plan?

How do *you* deal with Time? Are you even conscious of it? If you are, I bet you are constantly locked into either the future or the past. Relying on either memory or imagination.

Do you recognize these voices? "Once I get through this, I can have a drink . . . go on a vacation . . . retire." "I remember when I was young and practicing financial advisory was satisfying."

As you go to bed at midnight, are you thinking about waking up at 7:00 a.m. so that you can get to the office by 8:00 a.m. so that you can go to lunch by noon, because your software people will be there at 1:30 p.m. and you've got a full schedule and a new client scheduled at 2:30 p.m.?

Most of us are prisoners of the future or the past. While pinballing between the two, we miss the richest moments of our life—the present. Trapped forever in memory or imagination, we are strangers to the here and now. Our future is nothing more than an extension of our past, and the present is merely the background.

It's sobering to think that right now each of us is at a precise spot somewhere between the beginning of our Time (our birth) and the end of our Time (our death).

No wonder everyone frets about Time. What really terrifies us is that *we're using up our life and we can't stop it*.

It feels as if we're plummeting toward the end with nothing to break our free fall. Time is out of control! Understandably, this is horrifying, mostly because the real issue is not time with a small "t" but Death with a big "D."

From the depths of our existential anxiety, we try to put Time in a different perspective—all the while pretending we can manage it. We talk about Time as though it were something other than what it is. "Time is money," we announce, as though that explains it.

But what every financial advisor should know is that Time is life. And Time ends! Life ends!

The big, walloping, irresolvable problem is that *we don't know how much Time we have left.*

Do you feel the fear? Do you want to get over it?

Let's look at Time more seriously.

To fully grasp Time with a capital "T," you have to ask the Big Question: *How do I wish to spend the rest of my Time?*

Because I can assure you that if you don't ask that Big Question with a big "Q," you will forever be assailed by the little questions. You'll shrink the whole of your life to *this time* and *next time* and the *last time*—all the while wondering, *what time is it?*

It's like running around the deck of a sinking ship worrying about where you left the keys to your cabin.

You must accept that you have only so much Time; that you're using up that Time second by precious second. And that your Time, your life, is the most valuable asset you have. Of course, you can use your Time any way you want. But unless you choose to use it as richly, as rewardingly, as excitingly, as intelligently, as *intentionally* as possible, you'll squander it and fail to appreciate it.

Indeed, if you are oblivious to the value of your Time, you'll commit the single greatest sin: You will live your life unconscious of its passing you by.

Until you deal with Time with a capital "T," you'll worry about time with a small "t" until you have no Time—or life—left. Then your Time will be history . . . along with your life.

I can anticipate the question: If Time is the problem, why not just take on fewer clients? Well, that's certainly an option, but probably not necessary. I know a financial advisor with a small practice who sees four times as many clients as the average, yet the financial advisor and staff don't work long hours. How is it possible?

This financial advisor has a system. By using this expert system, the employees can do everything the financial advisor or his associate financial advisors would do—everything that isn't financial-advisor dependent.

Be versus Do

Remember when we all asked, "What do I want to be when I grow up?" It was one of our biggest concerns as children.

Notice that the question isn't, "What do I want to *do* when I grow up?" It's "What do I want to *be?*"

Shakespeare wrote, "To be or not to be." Not, "To do or not to do."

But when you grow up, people always ask you, "What do you *do?*" How did the question change from *being* to *doing?* How did we miss the critical distinction between the two?

Even as children, we sensed the distinction. The real question we were asking was not what we would end up *doing* when we grew up, but who we would *be*.

We were talking about a *life* choice, not a *work* choice. We instinctively saw it as a matter of how we spend our Time, not what we do *in* time.

Look to children for guidance. I believe that as children we instinctively saw Time as life and tried to use it wisely. As children, we wanted to make a life choice, not a work choice. As children, we didn't know—or care—that work had to be done on time, on budget.

Until you see Time for what it really is—your life span—you will always ask the wrong question.

Until you embrace the whole of your Time and shape it accordingly, you will never be able to fully appreciate the moment.

Until you fully appreciate every second that comprises Time, you will never be sufficiently motivated to live those seconds fully.

Until you're sufficiently motivated to live those seconds fully, you will never see fit to change the way you are. You will never take the quality and sanctity of Time seriously.

And unless you take the sanctity of Time seriously, you will continue to struggle to catch up with something behind you. Your frustrations will mount as you try to snatch the second that just whisked by.

If you constantly fret about time with a small "t," then big-"T" Time will blow right past you. And you'll miss the whole point, the real truth about Time: You can't manage it; you never could. You can only *live* it.

And so that leaves you with these questions: How do I live my life? How do I give significance to it? How can I be here now, in this moment?

Once you begin to ask these questions, you'll find yourself moving toward a much fuller, richer life. But if you continue to be caught up in the banal work you do every day, you're never going to find the time to take a deep breath, exhale, and be present in the now.

So, let's talk about the subject of *work*. But first, let's listen to what Michael Steranka has to say about time. ✤

What Time Do You Have?

Michael Steranka

It is the one thing we all have in common: We all are given the same twenty-four hours in a day. It's just that some people use them more wisely than others.

—Anonymous

I once asked my first general manager, Jim Adkins of the Chevy Chase, Maryland, office of New York Life: "What do I have to do to be a big producer in this business?"

Jim responded, "Mike, all you have to do is last."

Broadcaster Jim Lampley once had a similar conversation with actor Jack Nicholson, one of his closest friends. When Lampley asked Nicholson that same question about survival and having a long track record, Nicholson's response was, "In our industry, longevity is lovability."

Time is an important concept to keep in mind as you build your business. As you read this chapter, think about how you use your time. Are you moving too fast for your own good, or perhaps not fast enough?

Time is on your side. Young people are often too impatient to get to where they want to go. They can never get to their destination fast enough. Older people fall into a different trap, the "It's too late" trap, and they oftentimes can't seem to find the motivation to keep reaching higher.

So let's say this again: *time is on your side*. Even if you are older and you got a later start in your career, time works to your benefit because you have wisdom and a wealth of experiences at your side. If you are young, you still have the entire world open before you. What will you do with your wisdom? What will you do with all those possibilities?

Most people today are in too big of a hurry to get somewhere, usually because they're influenced by impatience or by anxiety. Strange enough, if they'd just slow down, they'll actually get to where they need to get to quicker. This is one of the most valuable lessons I've learned over my career.

Sometimes we're in danger of reaching a destination that we aren't supposed to reach right away and we find that we're not ready for it when we get there. Working toward a goal should never only be about that end goal. The journey toward that destination is what prepares us and strengthens us to be able to receive what's ahead. It's always better to arrive on time than to arrive too early or too late.

Rushing my clients will not help me provide good service for them. In order to maintain great relationships with my clients, I need to relax. Slow down. Ask questions. Instead of trying to guess what my clients will say, I need to listen and let the clients lead the pace of the conversation. If I do this and ask them the right questions, the clients will tell me everything about their life that is meaningful to them.

The beauty of our industry is that we can take the important personal stories and dreams that clients share with us and then help them actualize those dreams with their money. I believe there is no richer reward than seeing this play out. Clients have visions and they have money. As financial advisors, we bridge the two to help make those visions a reality.

I've been in meetings with clients where we bring in their adult children, and Mom and Dad tell their adult children what kind of legacy they plan to leave for them. My clients relay the sacrifices they made to attain this legacy during their children's lives, and oftentimes, an emotional conversation ensues. The meeting is joyful. Sometimes, it's teary. At least for the moment, Mom and Dad have embraced their mortality, and the children realize that they're not little kids anymore. The entire family recognizes that Mom and Dad are older and are giving the future serious consideration.

This kind of conversation absolutely cannot be rushed. You can't set a timer, tell the family to hug it out, and then move on to the next client. The amount of trust it takes for a roomful of adults to be this vulnerable in front of you can only develop over time.

You can't hurry up a sale or hurry up a relationship or hurry up the trust. The more you try to control time, the more it will backfire. Instead of trying to follow your own agenda, focus on doing the right thing for your clients. Stay in touch with them. Get to know them. Respect their pace.

We have gotten to know clients in such a way that some even bring gifts into the office. We get cookies and baked goods and letters—you name it. They appreciate what we do. Other times, clients will invite us to their parties or weddings or even to their funerals and other important events.

The way we view time and how much we value genuine relationships with clients evolves as the years go by. My opinion of what is important is quite different today from what it was twenty years ago. I am now better able to recognize how fragile life is. I remember my good friend, an attorney who did a lot of work with me. He recently retired and then became sick with Lou Gehrig's disease. Then he passed within a year. My friend's passing hit really close to home. We were close. We went on vacations together. And I'd assumed that I had at least ten or fifteen more years with him. But I really didn't. My friend was in great shape. He didn't drink, didn't smoke. He was a very serene kind of guy. But these things happen to anyone. We don't know why they happen, but they do. And the older and wiser you get, the more respect you have for time and the more you appreciate every moment instead of rushing toward the next one.

The best-laid plans don't prepare you for unexpected events. That friend, who happened to be a client of mine, was protected financially. But even if you are financially secure, other life circumstances occur. As you build your business and are eager to get to that next level, slow down. Really try to cherish every day that you have. I am so grateful for my life, my family, and my friends, my children, and everybody. I don't live my life in anxiety, worrying about how to get to that next moment. I stay present and I enjoy what I have now, and people always tell me that I'm smiling and having fun. It's true. I am. But we don't know when one visit to the doctor might change everything.

Your business and everything you own is valuable. But as you keep pace with where you're supposed to be, sober yourself from time to time by remembering that classic line: "How much money did he leave behind?" The answer will always be, "All of it."

Next, let's see what Michael E. Gerber has to say about work. ✤

CHAPTER

23

On the Subject
of Work

Michael E. Gerber

*As we learn we always change, and so our perception. This changed
perception then becomes a new Teacher inside each of us.*
—Hyemeyohsts Storm

I n the business world, as the saying goes, the entrepreneur knows something about everything, the technician knows everything about
something, and the switchboard operator just knows everything.

In a financial advisory practice, financial advisors see their natural
work as the work of the technician. The Supreme Technician. Often
to the exclusion of everything else.

After all, financial advisors get zero preparation working as a
manager and spend no time thinking as an entrepreneur—those
just aren't courses offered in today's schools and colleges of financial
advisory services. By the time they own their own financial advisory
practice, they're just doing it, doing it, doing it.

At the same time, they want everything—freedom, respect,
money. Most of all, they want to rid themselves of meddling bosses

and start their own practice. That way they can be their own boss and take home all the money. These financial advisors are in the throes of an entrepreneurial seizure.

Financial advisors who have been praised for their amazing analytical skills believe they have what it takes to run a financial advisory practice. It's not unlike the plumber who becomes a contractor because he's a great plumber. Sure, he may be a great plumber . . . but it doesn't necessarily follow that he knows how to build a practice that does this work.

It's the same for a financial advisor. So many of them are surprised to wake up one morning and discover that they're nowhere near as equipped for owning their own practice as they thought they were.

More than any other subject, work is the cause of obsessive-compulsive behavior by financial advisors.

Work. You've got to do it every single day.

Work. If you fall behind, you'll pay for it.

Work. There's either too much or not enough.

So many financial advisors describe work as what they do when they're busy. Some discriminate between the work they *could* be doing as financial advisors and the work they *should* be doing as financial advisors.

But according to the E-Myth, they're exactly the same thing. The work you *could* do and the work you *should* do as a financial advisor are identical. Let me explain.

Strategic Work versus Tactical Work

Financial advisors can do only two kinds of work: strategic work and tactical work.

Tactical work is easier to understand, because it's what almost every financial advisor does almost every minute of every hour of every day. It's called getting the job done. It's called doing business.

Tactical work includes filing, billing, answering the telephone, going to the bank, and seeing clients.

The E-Myth says that tactical work is all the work financial advisors find themselves doing in a financial advisory practice to *avoid* doing the strategic work.

"I'm too busy," most financial advisors will tell you.

"How come nothing goes right unless I do it myself?" they complain in frustration.

Financial advisors say these things when they're up to their ears in tactical work. But most financial advisors don't understand that if they had done more strategic work, they would have less tactical work to do.

Financial advisors are doing strategic work when they ask the following questions:

- Why am I a financial advisor?
- What will my practice look like when it's done?
- What must my practice look, act, and feel like in order for it to compete successfully?
- What are the key indicators of my practice?

Please note that I said financial advisors *ask* these questions when they are doing strategic work. I didn't say these are the questions they necessarily answer.

That is the fundamental difference between strategic work and tactical work. Tactical work is all about *answers*: How to do this. How to do that.

Strategic work, in contrast, is all about *questions*: What practice are we really in? Why are we in that practice? Who specifically is our practice determined to serve? When will I sell this practice? How and where will this practice be doing business when I sell it? And so forth.

Not that strategic questions don't have answers. Financial advisors who commonly ask strategic questions know that once they ask such a question, they're already on their way to *envisioning* the answer. Question and answer are part of a whole. You can't find the right answer until you've asked the right question.

Tactical work is much easier, because the question is always more obvious. In fact, you don't ask the tactical question; instead, the question arises from a result you need to get or a problem you need to solve. Billing a client is tactical work. Adjusting a client's portfolio is tactical work. Firing an employee is tactical work.

Tactical work is the stuff you do every day in your practice. Strategic work is the stuff you plan to do to create an exceptional practice/business/enterprise.

In tactical work, the question comes from *out there* rather than *in here*. The tactical question is about something *outside* of you, whereas the strategic question is about something *inside* of you.

The tactical question is about something you *need* to do, whereas the strategic question is about something you *want* to do. Want versus need.

If tactical work consumes you,

- you are always reacting to something outside of you;
- your practice runs you, you don't run it;
- your employees run you, you don't run them; and
- your life runs you, you don't run your life.

You must understand that the more strategic work you do, the more intentional your decisions, your practice, and your life become. *Intention* is the byword of strategic work.

Everything on the outside begins to serve you, to serve your vision, rather than forcing you to serve it. Everything you *need* to do is congruent with what you *want* to do. It means you have a vision, an aim, a purpose, a strategy, an *envisioned* result.

Strategic work is the work you do to *design* your practice, to design your life.

Tactical work is the work you do to *implement* the design created by strategic work.

Without strategic work, there is no design. Without strategic work, all that's left is keeping busy.

There's only one thing left to do. It's time to take action. And we'll do that right after Michael Steranka gives us his views on work. ❖

CHAPTER 24

The Reason Behind the Work

Michael Steranka

It's the work, the work, just the working life.

—Bruce Springsteen

The topic of this chapter brings to mind that classic Bruce Springsteen song, "The Factory." Although the song is about the grueling blue-collar life, its message resonates with all hardworking financial advisors.

But that's not the connotation of "work" I want to address in this chapter. The kind of "work" I want us to focus on is the kind that makes you excited about getting up in the morning; the kind you can't believe you get paid to do.

As you consider your work and your business, take a few steps back and return to discovering your unique ability. Your unique ability is the thing you would do for free. It's the passion embedded in your genetic makeup. The trick is to identify your unique ability and then figure out how you can get other people to pay you for executing your unique ability while you work at getting better at that unique ability. That's when you've hit the jackpot.

I love what I do and it's something I would do for free, and people somehow pay me substantial amounts of money to do it. When you approach a career this way, you are just like an outstanding athlete who loves to play baseball or basketball and gets paid to continue playing because he's that good at it. To that athlete, "work" is not a four-letter word. It's a three-letter word: fun! If I think of my work as a four-letter word and it's not fun to do, then I'm in the wrong line of business.

Once you decide what you like to do and figure out what you'd like to spend more time on, you can then delegate the things you don't like to do. When I took this approach and began to delegate the duties I didn't want, my "work" became much more enjoyable.

When I talk to my peers, many of them complain about different things and sulk over having to suffer through the grind. When I ask why they are so miserable, they say, "Because we have all this stuff to do."

I then ask them to tell me about all that stuff they have to do, and as they begin telling me, I say, "Why do you have to do that stuff? Are you good at any of it?"

They say, "No, not really. I actually have to force myself to be good at it."

Let's freeze this frame here. Bob is miserable. Bob has too much to do. Bob has to force himself to be good at these things he must do, and this kind of work is generally worth ten to twenty dollars an hour. Why is Bob still stuck doing this work for himself instead of paying somebody else to do it? If he were to pay somebody else, Bob would be happy, the person would get the work done and that person might even get it done in one-third the time it would have taken Bob, because Bob was forcing himself to be good at it in the first place.

When I began to delegate the four-letter work and keep what I considered the three-letter work for myself, I finally got to a point where sometimes 80 percent to 90 percent of my days are filled with fun. Of course, at least 10 percent of my days include the necessary "stuff," but I am definitely not in a place where I complain about the daily grind.

I love what I do. I meet with clients—new clients, old clients, prospective clients—and I spend my days talking to them. I discover my clients' stories. I find out what makes them tick. I come to understand how my clients view money. I learn how big their family is, to whom they want to leave money, why they want to leave that money, what they do for a living, and how they live their lives.

I'm fascinated by people and by the stories they tell. As I listen to my clients' stories, I often share some of my own, including personal stories or positive stories I have of past clients, which I might use to encourage my current clients. When my clients hear these stories, they might say, "I'd like for that to happen."

And that's when I love to say, "Well, I can show you how to make that happen." My client lights up, we have a productive conversation, and all of that counts as a day of work.

My clients and I sometimes talk about football. Or their children. We discuss where they're traveling to or the weather or golf or you name it. One of the perks of my job is being able to become integrated into a client's life.

This lifestyle is very different from the grind. Do you want to wake up and say, "Holy crap, it's only Tuesday?" Or do you want to wake up happy every day? It is possible to wake up happy every day. I take Fridays off, and I take two to three months off each year. But when I work, I work hard. Then when I'm off, I'm off. And I have a qualified and talented group of people to handle things when I'm not there. I owe this to systems, as taught by Michael E. Gerber.

Does it take work to get systems in place and establish the foundations for this lifestyle? Sure it does. But everything requires work. I've heard people quickly become discouraged and say, "That's too much work." But guess what? You're going to work anyway. You have to work. The difference is that as I've done with my work, I've put a system in place. But because you were discouraged, you're still just doing it, doing it, doing it.

When I tell people I'm flying to California for five days, they say, "You're always taking trips." That's right, I am. Then they say, "It must be nice." And I say, "Yes, it is!" But that's because I put the work in to make those vacations possible. I approach my business by asking myself how I can have more fun. It's liberating to be able to sketch out your own future. These are the fruits of laying out the right plans and the right systems for your business.

I once heard somebody say that being an entrepreneur gives you the ability to buy your freedom. It's true. We get to buy our freedom. And if we're successful long enough, we can buy our freedom permanently. In my opinion, the definition of that kind of freedom is the ability to do whatever you want, whenever you want, no matter what the circumstances, because you have the resources to do it. Only a very small percentage of people ever reach that point, but the good news is that it's possible. It's possible, and the people I've met who have accomplished this are extremely happy. They have good relationships and life is good.

I'm reminded of a story Earl Nightingale tells in one of his books. A woman approaches an opera singer after his performance and says, "I'd give anything to be able to sing the way you sing."

And the opera singer says, "No, you wouldn't. Because no, you didn't."

I've had people come up to me and say, "I would give anything to be a $50-million-a-year producer."

I look at them and say, "I don't think so." If those people really meant the words coming out of their mouths, they would have done it by now. Instead, some people say this to me two years in a row and still remain at the same production level.

I've also heard some people say, "But I don't want to work that hard." This is interesting to me because it's not that I'm working any harder than the next guy. We all have to work. We're both putting in the same time. So why is my compensation for my work a hundred times more than the next guy's? The answer is that I took the time to develop systems, figure out my unique ability, discover what I'm good at and what I enjoy, and delegate everything else.

When you delegate the things you don't like to do, you're freed to focus on the things you're good at; specifically, the things that will bring in the real revenue. And it makes your life a whole lot easier.

Don't be intimidated by the idea that this might be "more" work. It's not more work. It's better work. Let's see what Michael E. Gerber has to say about taking action. ✤

CHAPTER 25

On the Subject of Taking Action

Michael E. Gerber

Deliberation is the work of many men. Action, of one alone.
—Charles de Gaulle

It's time to get started, time to take action. Time to stop thinking about the old practice and start thinking about the new practice. It's not a matter of coming up with better practices; it's about reinventing the practice of financial advisory services.

And the financial advisor has to take personal responsibility for it.

That's you.

So sit up and pay attention!

You, the financial advisor, have to be interested. You cannot abdicate accountability for the practice of financial advisory services, the administration of financial advisory services, or the finance of financial advisory services.

Although the goal is to create systems into which financial advisors can plug reasonably competent people—systems that allow the practice to run without them—financial advisors must take responsibility for that happening.

I can hear the chorus now: "But we're financial advisors! We shouldn't have to know about this." To that I say: Whatever. If you don't give a flip about your practice, fine—close your mind to new knowledge and accountability. But if you want to succeed, then you'd better step up and take responsibility, and you'd better do it now.

All too often, financial advisors take no responsibility for the business of financial advisory services but instead delegate tasks without any understanding of what it takes to do them; without any interest in what their people are actually doing; without any sense of what it feels like to be at the front desk when a client comes in and has to wait for forty-five minutes; and without any appreciation for the entity that is creating their livelihood.

Financial advisors can open the portals of change in an instant. All you have to do is say, "I don't want to do it that way anymore." Saying it will begin to set you free—even though you don't yet understand what the practice will look like after it's been reinvented.

This demands an intentional leap from the known into the unknown. It further demands that you live there—in the unknown—for a while. It means discarding the past, everything you once believed to be true.

Think of it as soaring rather than plunging.

Thought Control

You should now be clear about the need to organize your thoughts first, then your business. Because the organization of your thoughts is the foundation for the organization of your business.

If we try to organize our business without organizing our thoughts, we will fail to attack the problem.

We have seen that organization is not simply time management. Nor is it people management. Nor is it tidying up desks or alphabetizing client files. Organization is first, last, and always cleaning up the mess of our minds.

By learning how to *think* about the practice of financial advisory services, by learning how to *think* about your priorities, and by learning how to *think* about your life, you'll prepare yourself to do righteous battle with the forces of failure.

Right thinking leads to right action—and now is the time to take action. Because it is only through action that you can translate thoughts into movement in the real world, and, in the process, find fulfillment.

So, first *think* about what you want to do. Then *do* it. Only in this way will you be fulfilled.

How do you put the principles we've discussed in this book to work in your financial advisory practice? To find out, accompany me down the path once more:

1. *Create a story about your practice.* Your story should be an idealized version of your financial advisory practice, a vision of what the preeminent financial advisor in your field should be and why. Your story must become the very heart of your practice. It must become the spirit that mobilizes it, as well as everyone who walks through the doors. Without this story, your practice will be reduced to plain work.

2. *Organize your practice so that it breathes life into your story.* Unless your practice can faithfully replicate your story in action, it all becomes fiction. In that case, you'd be better off not telling your story at all. And without a story, you'd be better off leaving your practice the way it is and just hoping for the best.

Here are some tips for organizing your financial advisory practice:

- Identify the key functions of your practice.
- Identify the essential processes that link those functions.
- Identify the results you have determined your practice will produce.
- Clearly state in writing how each phase will work.

Take it step by step. Think of your practice as a program, a piece of software, a system. It is a collaboration, a collection of processes dynamically interacting with one another.

Of course, your practice is also people.

3. *Engage your people in the process.* Why is this the third step rather than the first? Because, contrary to the advice most business experts will give you, you must never engage your people in the process until you yourself are clear about what you intend to do.

The need for consensus is a disease of today's addled mind. It's a product of our troubled and confused times. When people don't know what to believe in, they often ask others to tell them. To ask is not to lead but to follow.

The prerequisite of sound leadership is first to know where you wish to go.

And so, "What do I want?" becomes the first question; not, "What do *they* want?" In your own practice, the vision must first be yours. To follow another's vision is to abdicate your personal accountability, your leadership role, your true power.

In short, the role of leader cannot be delegated or shared. And without leadership, no financial advisory practice will ever succeed.

Despite what you have been told, *win-win* is a secondary step, not a primary one. The opposite of *win-win* is not necessarily *they lose.*

Let's say "they" can win by choosing a good horse. The best choice will not be made by consensus. "Guys, what horse do you think we should ride?" will always lead to endless and worthless discussions. By the time you're done jawing, the horse will have already left the post.

Before you talk to your people about what you intend to do in your practice and why you intend to do it, you need to reach agreement with yourself.

It's important to know (1) *exactly* what you want, (2) how you intend to proceed, (3) what's important to you and what isn't, and (4) what you want the practice to be and how you want it to get there.

Once you have that agreement, it's critical that you engage your people in a discussion about what you intend to do and why. Be clear—both with yourself and with them.

The Story

The story is paramount because it is your vision. Tell it with passion and conviction. Tell it with precision. Never hurry a great story. Unveil it slowly. Don't mumble or show embarrassment. Never apologize or display false modesty. Look your audience in the eyes and tell your story as though it is the most important one they'll ever hear about business. Your business. The business into which you intend to pour your heart, your soul, your intelligence, your imagination, your time, your money, and your sweaty persistence.

Get into the storytelling zone. Behave as though it means everything to you. Show no equivocation when telling your story.

These tips are important because you're going to tell your story over and over—to clients, to new and old employees, to financial advisors, to associate financial advisors, and to your family and friends. You're going to tell it at your church or synagogue; to your card-playing or fishing buddies; and to organizations such as Kiwanis, Rotary, YMCA, Hadassah, and Boy Scouts.

There are few moments in your life when telling a great story about a great business is inappropriate.

If it is to be persuasive, you must love your story. Do you think Walt Disney loved his Disneyland story? Or Ray Kroc his McDonald's story? What about Dave Smith at Federal Express? Or Debbie Fields at Mrs. Fields Cookies? Or Tom Watson Jr. at IBM?

Do you think these people loved their stories? Do you think others loved (and *still* love) to hear them? I daresay *all* successful entrepreneurs have loved the story of their business. Because that's what true entrepreneurs do. They tell stories that come to life in the form of their business.

Remember: A great story never fails. A great story is always a joy to hear.

In summary, you first need to clarify, both for yourself and for your people, the *story* of your practice. Then you need to detail the *process* your practice must go through to make your story become reality.

I call this the business development process. Others call it re-engineering, continuous improvement, reinventing your practice, or total quality management.

Whatever you call it, you must take three distinct steps to succeed:

- *Innovation.* Continue to find better ways of doing what you do.
- *Quantification.* Once that is achieved, quantify the impact of these improvements on your practice.
- *Orchestration.* Once these improvements are verified, orchestrate this better way of running your practice so that it becomes your standard, to be repeated time and again.

In this way, the system works—no matter who's using it. And you've built a practice that works consistently, predictably, systematically. A practice you can depend on to operate exactly as promised, every single time.

Your vision, your people, your process—all linked.

A superior financial advisory practice is a creation of your imagination, a product of your mind. So fire it up and get started! Now let's listen to what Michael Steranka has to say about taking action. ✤

CHAPTER 26

Taking Action

Michael Steranka

*I never told women my cosmetics would make them beautiful, but I
always gave them hope.*

—Elizabeth Arden

Hope is the magic elixir, and taking action is what gives me hope. Throughout this book, I've hammered home the fine points of how to E-Myth your financial advisory business. Now that the "how" is in place, I want to spend this last chapter discussing the "why." Why should we take action? Why apply the E-Myth system to your business at all?

The fuel that drives me is hope. A day when I have five new appointments is a day that gives me hope. These new appointments give me hope because I've seen enough of people's financial situations to know what incredibly positive effects financial advisors can have on people's lives. I bear great news: In this business, you will never run out of people to help. If I ran out of people to help, I would stop enjoying my work.

I am the most charged after a day of meetings with prospective clients and with existing clients who have been with me for years. It is rejuvenating to put names and faces to the people I serve and be reminded that this line of work is, in fact, a service.

I remember one particular couple I worked with. The husband was about to turn eighty, and his wife, seventy-seven. This couple said to me, "We're slowing down. But you've looked after us for the last fifteen years and we're so grateful that you've kept us. We know we're not a big account. But we've watched you grow and we truly appreciate you in our lives."

Heartfelt messages like that from long-term clients are priceless. That couple reminded me all over again why I do what I do. They gave me even more hope so that I can continue to take actions in the right direction.

Whether I am meeting people for the first time or meeting people I've helped numerous times, my focus is on, frankly, pouring out love for them. I always keep the client's best interest at heart and always make sure that my suggestions are open-ended. If I've discovered something that can really help a client, I'll say, "Do you think you can do this? I just went to this conference where I saw this, so let me give you one of these advance-planning things to think about." I like to tell clients that I'm giving them something to think about. Then some of them go home and actually think about those things and if they still remember it the next time they come in, we discuss it, and then I help them implement it.

What might give a newer producer hope is a sale. Or it might be the opportunity to meet with a prospective client or the chance to make a presentation that is expected to end in a close. I've seen this chain of events countless of times, thanks to my systems, and now, what gives me hope is meeting with clients and focusing on what they need. Securing a sale isn't the thing that drives me anymore, because I know that we're doing enough to always be in front of enough people. We will never run out of people to serve.

Like anything else, getting to this point takes some time. But even that development process is part of the fun. For example, as of this writing, our company plans to kick off a series of outings for our clients. For fourteen weeks, we're going to take twenty people a week out for golf at a private club. That should be a lot of fun, and should give most of the clients a chance to come out at least once or twice. I hope they will bring a friend or two with them to introduce to us. I'm giving out rounds of golf at a sophisticated club, but people like it. Being able to take action like this for my clients gives me hope.

Think about the various things that bring hope into your life. For me, developing as a well-rounded person gives me hope. Hiring a personal trainer, hiring a nutritionist, and doing whatever I need to do to stay in shape all give me hope. Following my faith gives me hope. Doing charity work to help people outside my business gives me hope. My wife and I enjoy giving away our time, and sometimes we enjoy giving away our money to causes. Being able to open up our house for an event or providing scholarships also gives me hope.

Hope is powerful because it goes beyond the visible and propels you into the future, which contains possibilities and realized dreams. If you have hope, you keep going. People are what keep me going and people are what give me hope.

One of the kindest Christmas cards I ever received was from a woman who was extremely down and out. Life gave this woman a lot of challenges, and I was able to provide her some transportation on a permanent basis. One Christmas, she gave me a Christmas card from her and her children. It was a handmade card and it was nothing too fancy. But it was filled with so much warmth and love. It was absolutely the best Christmas card I ever got. Even talking about this simple card makes me tear up. This kind of reward will always outweigh any monetary compensation for my work.

When you're doing the right thing and the stars align and you know that you're exactly where you're supposed to be in life, relish it. It doesn't get any better than that.

In order to get the most out of life, remember to approach situations from a position of abundance. Most people operate from a negative platform. They come from a place of "lack," and they complain that there aren't enough prospects out there. But with the right mindset, you will see that there will always be more people to serve than you can ever handle. The question that will make your business successful and enjoyable isn't "What can I get from people?" but "What can I give to people?"

The most successful business coaches have said this for years: Provide the service. Provide the service and the money will come. Be successful first. Be successful in your mind and give of your services as though you've already made it. The more you serve and the more you offer, the more people will be attracted to you. The money will follow as a result.

The mentality of the highly successful, hopeful individual is a combination of thinking in terms of abundance and thinking in terms of service. When you couple that combination with hard work, intelligence, proper planning, and the right systems, the final question you'll find yourself asking is "How could I *not* succeed?" ♣

AFTERWORD

Michael E. Gerber

For more than three decades, I've applied the E-Myth principles I've shared with you in this book to the successful development of thousands of small businesses throughout the world. Many have been financial advisory practices.

Few rewards are greater than seeing these E-Myth principles improve the work and lives of so many people. Those rewards include seeing these changes:

- Lack of clarity—clarified
- Lack of organization—organized
- Lack of direction—shaped into a path that is clearly, lovingly, passionately pursued
- Lack of money or money poorly managed—money understood instead of coveted; created instead of chased; wisely spent or invested instead of squandered
- Lack of committed people—transformed into a cohesive community working in harmony toward a common goal; discovering each other and themselves in the process; all the while expanding their understanding, their know-how, their interest, their attention

After working with so many financial advisors, I know that a practice can be much more than what most become. I also know that nothing is preventing you from making your practice all that it can be. It takes only desire and the perseverance to see it through.

In this book—the next in the E-Myth Expert series—the E-Myth principles have been complemented and enriched by stories from Michael Steranka, a real-life financial advisor who has put these principles to use in his practice. Michael had the desire and perseverance to achieve success beyond his wildest dreams. Now you, too, can join him.

I hope this book has helped you clear your vision and set your sights on a very bright future.

To your practice!

ABOUT THE AUTHORS

Michael E. Gerber

Michael E. Gerber is the legend behind the E-Myth series of books, which includes *The E-Myth Revisited*, *E-Myth Mastery*, *The E-Myth Manager*, *The E-Myth Enterprise* and *Awakening the Entrepreneur Within*. Collectively, his books have sold millions of copies worldwide. He is the founder of In the Dreaming Room™, a 2½-day process to awaken the entrepreneur within, and Origination, which trains facilitators to assist entrepreneurs in growing "turnkey" businesses. He is chairman of the Michael E. Gerber Companies. A highly sought-after speaker and consultant, he has trained more than 70,000 businesses in his career. Michael lives with his wife, Luz Delia, in Carlsbad, California.

ABOUT THE AUTHORS

Michael Steranka

Michael Steranka is founder and CEO of Retirement Planning Services, Inc. With more than twenty years of experience, Michael is an expert in the financial services field. Through his mentoring and coaching program, Michael advises other financial advisors on the rise. He is among the top producers specializing in annuity financial advisement in the United States and is a sought-after speaker and consultant. He lives in Millersville, Maryland.

ABOUT THE SERIES

The E-Myth Expert series brings Michael E. Gerber's proven E-Myth philosophy to a wide variety of different professional practice areas. The E-Myth, short for "Entrepreneurial Myth," is simple: too many small businesses fail to grow because their leaders think like technicians, not entrepreneurs. Gerber's approach gives small enterprise leaders practical, proven methods that have already helped transform more than 70,000 businesses. Let the E-Myth Expert series boost your professional practice today!

Books in the series include:
The E-Myth Attorney
The E-Myth Accountant
The E-Myth Optometrist
The E-Myth Chiropractor
The E-Myth Financial Advisor

Forthcoming books in the series include:
The E-Myth Landscape Contractor
The E-Myth Rainmaker
The E-Myth Real Estate Investor
The E-Myth Real Estate Brokerage
... and 300 more industries and professions

Learn more at: www.michaelegerber.com/co-author

Have you created an E-Myth enterprise? Would you like to become a Co-Author of an E-Myth book in your industry? Go to www.michaelegerber.com/co-author.

THE MICHAEL E. GERBER
ENTREPRENEUR'S LIBRARY
It Keeps Growing...

Thank you for reading another E-Myth Vertical book.

Who do you know who is an expert in their industry?

Who has applied The E-Myth to the improvement of their
practice as Michael Steranka has?

Who can add immense value to others in his or her industry
by sharing what he or she has learned?

Please share this book with that individual and share that individual with us.

We at Michael E. Gerber Companies are determined to transform the state
of small business and entrepreneurship worldwide. *You can help.*

To find out more, email us at Michael E. Gerber Partners, at
gerber@michaelegerber.com.

To find out how *YOU* can apply the E-Myth to *YOUR* practice,
contact us at gerber@michaelegerber.com.

Thank you for living your Dream, and changing the world.

Michael E. Gerber, Co-Founder/Chairman
Michael E. Gerber Companies™
Creator of The E-Myth Evolution™
P.O. Box 131195, Carlsbad, CA 92013
760-752-1812 O • 760-752-9926 F
gerber@michaelegerber.com
www.michaelegerber.com

Join The Evolution^{SM}

Find the latest updates:
www.michaelegerber.com

Attend the Dreaming Room Trainings
www.michaelegerber.com

Listen to the Michael E. Gerber Radio Show
www.blogtalkradio.com/michaelegerber

Watch the latest videos
www.youtube.com/michaelegerber

Connect on LinkedIn
www.linkedin.com/in/michaelegerber

Connect on Facebook
www.facebook.com/MichaelEGerberCo

Follow on Twitter
http://twitter.com/michaelegerber

CPSIA information can be obtained at www.ICGtesting.com
Printed in the USA
LVOW120012150313

324075LV00002BA/10/P